Therefore,
Being-Gods
drove out the person

And
placed at the east
of the Garden
of Eden
a Cherubim
and
a flaming sword

Which
turned around
to guard the Way
to the Tree of Life.

(Genesis 3:24)

The Second Coming
of
Eve, Abraham, Buddha, and Jesus

Their Lost Way
to
Personal and Global Peace

Robert W. North, PhD

THE SECOND COMING
OF
EVE, ABRAHAM, BUDDHA, AND JESUS

Their Lost Way
to
Personal and Global Peace

Copyright © 2020 by Robert W. North

All rights reserved. No part of this book may be used or reproduced by any means, graphic, electronic, or mechanical, including photocopying, recording, taping or by any information storage retrieval system without the written permission of the publisher except in the case of brief quotations embodied in critical articles and reviews.

Because of the dynamic nature of the Internet, any Web addresses or links contained in this book may have changed since publication and may no longer be valid.

ISBN-13: 978-1-64945-960-2

Cover design by Nada Orlic:
https://www.nadaorlic.com/

7771—The Way of the Soul
www.7771.org
San Diego, California

PREFACE

THE COVER

On the cover, you see the Tree of the Knowledge of Life. It is central to the Adam and Eve story which is the second chapter of the first book of the Bible. The four figures on the cover represent Eve, Abraham, Buddha, and Jesus. They are marching to the tree to eat its "fruit." They are doing that because a core command in the Garden story told them to do that if they want to be spiritually and psychologically alive all day, every day. In this book, you will read their words, which teach us how to imitate their "way" to living a fulfilled life.

INTRODUCTION

Eve: I call the author of the Adam and Eve Story "Eve" because she is an important, positive, transformational figure in the composition.

Abraham: Most of Genesis narrates the journey of Abraham and his progeny to what has been called the "Promised Land." Neither historical scholars nor theologians know the identity of the author of these passages. In this book, I will call the composer "Abraham."[1]

Buddha: His given name was Siddhartha Gautama; his title was "the Buddha" (the Enlightened One). He was born around 480 BCE and died around 400 BCE. He lived and taught in the Northeast of ancient India.

We do not possess the actual sayings of this great wise man. Three hundred years after he died, people recorded in writing what previous generations had memorized. One of the most significant compilations of his words is *The Dhammapada*,[1] from which we will quote. As you read his words, you will see that he also knew about and expanded upon the Garden of Eden story.

Jesus: Jesus lived 400 years after Buddha, from about 4 BCE to about 30 CE. To understand his insights, we will be quoting from the New

Testament and my translation of *The Gospel of Thomas*.[2] In this book, you will examine texts that show that Jesus expanded upon and explained the insights of Eve, Abraham, and Buddha.

What do Eve, Abraham, Buddha, and Jesus Offer Us Today?

To establish the basis for answering that question, permit me to ask you, the reader, other questions?

1. Do you wish that there existed a single way that everyone on the planet could live such that we would have no more religious or secular conflicts?

2. Do you wish that there existed a single way that everyone on the planet could live (including atheists) that would be both a mental and a spiritual health development system?

3. Do you wish that you knew the ancient secret for resolving all of your worries, regrets, and anxieties?

If your answer is "yes" to these questions, you know what Eve, Abraham, Buddha, and Jesus offer us today. They articulated a revolutionary "way" that provides most of what you and I desire and a lot more!

Background

My name is Robert North. When I was in a Catholic Jesuit seminary for priests, I began to suspect that Jesus was more of a therapist than a theologian. I arrived at that conclusion because none of the dogmatic statements in the Nicene Creed, which is the foundation of Christianity, are found in Jesus' compositions. For example, he never told people to believe in his resurrection, that he was born of a virgin, that he died to save us from original sin, or that he was the only son of God. Those are all statements made by people after he died. Instead of preaching dogmas, Jesus used sayings and parables to teach people how to live a fulfilled life.

I was more convinced that Jesus would not be a Christian when I read the letters of Paul the Apostle. He did not preach even one of Jesus' sayings and parables. Instead, he invented his version of Jesus' message, which today is the foundation of Christian theology.

My confusion escalated when I read in the Gospel of Mark (1:14) that Jesus taught "the gospel of God," which the Book of Acts (9:1-2) describes as a "way."

MARK 1:14	ACTS 9:1-2
And after the delivering up of John Jesus came into Galilee And he preached the **gospel of God.**	Indeed Paul, still breathing threats and murder against the disciples of the Lord, went to the high priest and asked him for letters to the synagogues in Damascus in order that he might bring bound to Jerusalem any whom he found who belonged to the **Way**, both men and women.

When I asked theologians and clergy for an explanation of Jesus' "gospel" and "way," I discovered that there existed no consensus about the meaning of those two terms. So I asked myself, "How could Christians claim to follow Jesus if they did not know what he was preaching and doing?"

After six years, I left the Jesuits and Christianity, but not my passion for understanding Jesus' "gospel" and "way." That quest led me to enroll in the University of Florida graduate program in Counseling. I did that because the professors and students were studying how people could achieve high levels of emotional and mental health, which seemed to be Jesus' goal.

After obtaining my Ph.D. and while working as an organizational counselor, I joined informally with other scripture scholars to:

1. Discover the real Jesus, and

2. To discover how the Biblical authors organized their texts to explain their meanings.[3] Scholars have recognized that these authors were following literary rules that history has lost.[2] I made their discovery a co-passion hoping that these rules would disclose Jesus' gospel and way.

My breakthrough in understanding both the ancient, oral literary rules and the meaning of Jesus' "gospel" and "way" came when I studied the *Gospel of Thomas*. It is a pre-third century CE Semitic text discovered buried in Egypt in 1945. The opening sentence proclaims that Jesus was the author of the book. The second sentence states that his disciple, Thomas, was the scribe. In the margin of one page, a copyist called the work, the *Gospel of Thomas*; however, no one knows if that is how it was originally titled.

In the relatively few years since the discovery of the *Gospel of Thomas*, no one has found the key to the organization of the book. To those who studied the work, it appeared to consist of 114 sayings arranged almost randomly, although someone organized the sayings around keywords.[4]

Gradually over ten years of study of the *Gospel of Thomas*, I determined that:

1. The Semitic authors for at least a thousand years before the Common Era carefully followed highly sophisticated oral and written literary rules that apply to most of the Bible, to the *Gospel of Thomas*, and to other Semitic works. I called this ancient literary method, "Semitic Parallelism;"[5]

2. Translators, theologians, linguists, historians, and clergy have not been using Semitic Parallelism to lay out and interpret Semitic texts. That fact calls into question their conclusions over the past 2000 years;

3. The *Gospel of Thomas* is a highly organized 21-Chapter Book of 131 wisdom poems;[2]

4. Jesus was the probable author of the *Gospel of Thomas*, and

5. That no one could understand Jesus' "gospel" and "way" without the information in the *Gospel of Thomas.*

I then applied the Semitic Parallelism rule to much of the Bible and discovered that:

1. Jesus' gospel was expanding upon and explaining the "way" of Eve, Abraham and Buddha,

2. This "way" is an alternative to and incompatible with dogma-based religions,

3. This "way" provides the mental and spiritual development secrets that we seek,

4. This "way" resolves religious conflicts and most secular conflicts,

5. Moses, Paul the Apostle, Mohammed, and the theologians who based their insights on the writings of these three founders of religions misunderstood this "way." (Many scholars agree that Paul, not Jesus, founded Christianity).[6,7]

I then turned my attention to the study of the early texts that best reflected the "way" of Buddha. I discovered that he was expanding upon and explaining the same lost "way" that Eve, Abraham, and Jesus taught. (Jesus adopted many of Buddha's metaphors).

My application of Semitic Parallelism to the Bible also showed that:

1. The Bible should not be laid out in newspaper columns like we see today.

2. The Biblical authors organized their works to tell us their chapter and section breaks (which differ from those in our current Bibles).

3. The organization of most texts disclose the authors' meanings for metaphors and sections. In other words, many Biblical books contain an internal dictionary and commentary.

4. We can determine where copyists have deleted and inserted text. As a result, we largely can reconstruct the original document.

5. Many sections and books of the Bible should be read as allegories, not as historical narratives. When approached this way, our understanding of the text changes, sometimes radically. For example, many authors were against indoctrinating religions and taught an alternative **Way**—the same **Way** that Eve, Abraham, Buddha, and Jesus preached. In a more specific example, when read as an allegory, the meaning of Abraham's Covenant, which is the foundation of Israel's claim to its territory, alters tremendously with international implications.

CONCLUSION

The invention of Semitic Parallelism resulted in a literary genre comparable to, and perhaps, more sophisticated than those we use today. We must learn to use it if we intend to understand the ancient Semitic authors.

PEER REVIEW

All of these discoveries have been verified informally by my colleagues and editors. However, it will be many years before other scholars finish formally critiquing the findings. That leaves me with two choices: I can withhold publishing until the formal reviews have been completed, or I can publish immediately so that everyone can learn about, apply, and verify the discoveries. I am choosing the latter course.

YOUR ROLE

We present in this book the words of Eve, Abraham, Buddha, and Jesus in the way that they organized them to be heard and read. Your job is to challenge them and us and to arrive at your conclusions—and, and if you wish, to present your ideas to the world on our web site (**www.7771.org**). To participate in that way, you will need to be very open. Many of the ideas of Eve, Abraham, Buddha, and Jesus are not only counter-intuitive, but they probably will challenge your current beliefs—as they have done ours.'

END NOTES

1. See Appendix Two for notes about the translations.

2. North, Robert W: *The Gospel of Thomas—The Original 21-Chapter Poetic Arrangement,* 2017, The Soul Way Press. (The Gospel of Thomas was discovered buried in Egypt in 1945. Our present text dates to the 4th century; however, the original was composed much earlier. In the Appendix, I present 14 reasons to believe that Jesus left us his Gospel).

3. John Breck, *The Shape of Biblical Language,* Crestwood, N.Y., St. Vladimir's Seminary Press, 1994.

4. Stephen. J. Patterson, *The Gospel of Thomas and Jesus,* Sanoma, CA; Polebridge Press, 1993.

5. North, Robert William; *The Semitic Secret—How Semitic Authors Organized Their Works to Include a Dictionary, Commentary, and a Method of Determining Scribal Errors.* The Soul Way Press, 2020.

6. Wilson, Barrie, *How Jesus Became a Christian,* First St. Martin Press, 2009.

7. North, Robert William: *The Messiah's Unrealized Revolution,* The Soul Way Press, 2017 (This book compares the personal/spiritual development theory of Jesus and Paul the Apostle).

CONTENTS

Preface	v
Chapter One: Our Two Ways to Live	1
Introduction	1
Abraham Maslow and the Two Ways	2
Martin Buber and the Two Ways	4
Buddha and the Two Ways to Live	10
Jesus and the Two Ways to Live	13
The Foundational Question	14
Summary	15
Chapter Two: The Garden of Eden Allegory: Our Birth	19
Introduction	19
Types of Allegories	20
What Are We Going to Call "God?"	24
Jesus vs. Christian Theology	30
Buddha and Being Yourself	33
Chapter Three: The Garden of Eden Allegory: The Garden Command	41
Knowing the Sublime	48
Child Development	49
Chapter Four: The Garden of Eden Allegory: Our Woman	53
Our Feminine and Masculine	55
The Creation of Our Woman	55
Jesus Taught the Garden Command	58
Psychological Healing	66
Chapter Five: The Garden of Eden Allegory: How We Obtain Free Choice	67
Summary	73
Chapter Six: The Garden of Eden Allegory: How We Sin	75
Jesus Mental Health Secret	77
Jesus and the Source of Division and Its Remedy	90
Summary	93

Chapter Seven: The Garden of Eden Allegory: We Testify in the Garden Court 95

Summary 101

Chapter Eight: The Garden of Eden Allegory: Spirit Sentences Us 103

Introduction 103

The Snake's Punishment 103

The Woman's Punishment 106

The Man's Punishment 107

Chapter Nine: The Garden of Eden Allegory: Spirit Banishes Us 111

Introduction 111

We Gain Our Dignity 111

Our Punishment 112

Garden of Eden Summary 121

Chapter Ten: The Abraham Allegory: The Covenant 123

Chapter Eleven: The Abraham Allegory: Our Guide 135

Chapter Twelve: The Abraham Allegory: Circumcise Yourself 147

Chapter Thirteen: The Abraham Allegory: Sacrifice Your Isaac 155

Chapter Fourteen: The Jacob Allegory 165

Chapter Fifteen: The Joseph Allegory 171

Chapter Sixteen: The Moses Allegory: I Am Who I Am 177

Chapter Seventeen: The Moses Allegory: Choose Your God 183

Chapter Eighteen: The Moses Allegory Divide Your Sea 187

Chapter Nineteen: The Moses Allegory: Know Inspiration with the Tree of Life 195

Chapter Twenty: The Moses Allegory: Continually Eat Inspiration 199

Chapter Twenty-One: The Moses Allegory: Beware of the
Leader Who Becomes a Pharaoh   205

Chapter Twenty-Two: The Moses Allegory:
Don't Bow to Pharaohs   209

Chapter Twenty-Three: The Moses Allegory: Make Human
Laws Secondary to Natural Laws   219

Chapter Twenty-Four: The Moses Allegory: Beware of
Religious Tyrants   231

Chapter Twenty-Five: The Moses Allegory: We Are Punished
and Rewarded Every Moment   235

Chapter Twenty-Six: The Joshua Allegory: Follow Joshua   239

Chapter Twenty-Seven: The Saul and David Allegory:
Do Not Divide Your Loyalties   249

Chapter Twenty-Eight: The Saul and David Allegory:
Israelites Defeat Goliaths   261

Chapter Twenty-Nine: The Saul and David Allegory:
Do Not Love Unwisely   269

Chapter Thirty: The King David Allegory: Remain
Humble and Single   275

Chapter Thirty-One: The King David Allegory: Follow the
Covenant in Your Ark (Heart)   283

Chapter Thirty-Two: The Book Summary   291

Appendix One: Addendum to Chapter Twenty-Three   297

Appendix Two: Abel and David vs. Cain and Saul   299

Appendix Three: David and the Torah Laws   303

Appendix Four: Notes About the Translations   307

Acknowledgments   309

CHAPTER ONE

OUR TWO WAYS
TO LIVE

INTRODUCTION

As you read in the Preface,[1] Eve, Abraham, Buddha, and Jesus taught that beyond what appears to be many ways that people can live, there are, according to them, *two and only two ways*. You will see from their writings that one Way results in what they call the experience of "darkness," and the other, the experience of "light."

For example, in the Dhammapada (Ch. 6), Buddha said:

> *The Master*
> *abandons the Dark Way*
> *for the Light Way.*

In this book, you will read that Eve, Abraham, and Jesus used similar, but varied expressions to describe the two ways to live. To integrate their terms, I will call the two ways: The *Mind Way* and the *Soul Way*. As you read further in this book, you will understand the justification for my terminology.

CONTEMPORARY DESCRIPTIONS OF THE TWO WAYS

You, the reader, may not have stopped and reflected on the differences between the Mind (Dark) Way and the Soul (Light) Way, but two contemporary men did. One was the psychologist, Abraham Maslow, and the other, a Jewish theologian/philosopher, Martin Buber.

---

[1] *Preface:* You, the reader, will have difficulty understanding the rest of the book if you did not read the Preface.

Abraham Maslow and the Two Ways

Abraham Maslow focused his research on two opposing ways to live, which he called "The Normal Way" and "Experience," and "The Peak Way" and "Experience." His writings about them were among the forces that led to the creation of Transpersonal Psychology.

Transpersonal therapists seek to teach people how to live in the Peak Way all day, every day. He described people who do that as being *"self-actualized"* because the more that people live on the Peak Way, the more they become fulfilled and independent.

Maslow interviewed many self-actualized people. Most said that they experienced a Peak Experience when they went aside from their normal activities and environment to one that was peacefully and beautifully different. They all described the differences between the Normal Way and the Peak Way in terms such as the following:

The Normal Way and Experience	The Peak Way and Experience
I am on a roller-coaster emotional life.	I am still, full of love and joy.
I feel dead.	I feel alive.
I am in my mind and don't feel one with my soul.	I am one with my soul primarily, and my mind secondarily.
I am divided from myself, others, and from nature.	I am one with myself, others, and nature.
I live from my mind in the past and future.	I live from my soul in the "now moment."
I conditionally love me and others.	I unconditionally love me and others.
I feel disempowered.	I feel empowered.
I worry because I do not know what the future will bring.	I don't worry because by living in the moment, I know what steps will lead me to fulfillment.
I act with effort.	I act effortlessly.

The Normal Way And Experience	The Peak Way And Experience
I manufacture ideas in my mind.	Ideas flow through me naturally from my soul.
I love with difficulty.	Love comes easily.
I am afraid of intimacy.	I can easily be intimate.
I lack self-confidence	I am self-confident
I worry about meeting the expectation of others.	I am peacefully independent of others.
I am unconscious of my feelings, thoughts, and actions and their impact on myself and others	I am conscious of my feelings, thoughts, and actions, and their impact on myself and others.

In the above chart, you will notice that when we are on the Normal Way, we live in and from our minds, not in and from our souls. Our minds impose ideas on reality. Our souls experience reality. Our minds divide us from ourselves and others. Our souls unite us with ourselves and others. Consequently, in this book we call the two Ways the *Mind Way* and the *Soul Way*. That distinction seems to best describe the two Ways of Eve, Abraham, Buddha, and Jesus.

GRAPHIC SUMMARY OF THE TWO WAYS

The Mind Way (The Normal Way)

A person primarily lives from his mental ideas and beliefs.

→ **Results in**

The Dark (Normal) Experience

(An unfulfilled life)

The Soul Way (The Peak Way)

A person primarily lives from his soul-known inspiration.

→ **Results in**

The Light (Peak) Experience

(A fulfilled life)

MARTIN BUBER AND THE TWO WAYS

Just as Abraham Maslow discovered the two Ways to live, Martin Buber also did. He noticed that a person might choose to have an "I-It relationship" with someone or something or an "I-Thou relationship" with the same person, object, or event. Let me explain Buber's fascinating insights with two personal examples.

In the past, I went to some gatherings of people that included drinks and hors d'oeuvres. When there, I manipulated my words and actions to fit what others expected. As a result, I felt distant from myself and them. I was not me. Buber would say that I had established a dysfunctional "I-It Relationship" with myself and others.

He calls it an "I-It Relationship" because I experienced myself and others as objects, not as human beings. I did not soul-connect with each person. Instead, I pretended to be intimate with them. However, my soul knew that I was not real and told me that by filling my body with anxiety and stress. That showed itself when I forced my words and my laughter.

More recently, I have changed and am usually my real self with others. Buber would say that I am learning to establish "I-Thou Relationships" with them. I honestly say what I mean and accept the consequences. My words and laughter flow from the heart. As a result, I experience more intimacy with others.

The following chart presents how Martin Buber described these Two Ways to live:

THE I-IT RELATIONSHIP OR THE MIND WAY AND THE RESULTING DARK EXPERIENCE	THE I-THOU RELATIONSHIP OR THE SOUL WAY AND THE RESULTING LIGHT EXPERIENCE
I am false.	I am the real me.
I manipulate myself to be accepted by others.	I invite others to love or not love me.
I am distant from myself and others.	I am one with myself and others.
I am anxious, worried, and stiff.	I am at peace and relaxed.
I see myself and the other person as objects.	I see the other person as a living being, like me.
Deep-down, I am miserable and alone.	I am peacefully at one with myself and others, even when I am alone.

WORKBOOK

This book is both a textbook and a workbook. Some of you readers may be tempted to skip the workbook exercises and focus on what you consider the "meat." You may find that to be a mistake. Let me explain why.

The Soul Way is a radically different way to live. All of us have a difficult time grasping and living its tenets because society today teaches us to use Mind Way principles and logic to understand everything. To understand and live the Soul Way, one must suspend the Mind Way and leap into what often appears to be foolishness.

For those of you who want to ensure that you understand the insights of Maslow, Buber, Eve, Abraham, Buddha, and Jesus, we will present exercises that will test your ability to apply their Soul Way principles and logic to your life.

Exercise:

Please read Maslow's and Buber's above descriptions of the two Ways and decide to what degree you are generally on the Mind Way and to what degree you live on the Soul Way. After you do that, you will get more out of the following sections.

You, the Reader, and the Two Ways to Live

Below, I will ask you to recall times when you may have transitioned from the Mind Way to the Soul Way. By reflecting on those events, you will see that you are no different from the people mentioned.

Vacations: Again, let me be personal, and then, you decide if my experience matches yours.

When I go on vacation, I always choose to go to a beautiful place. When I first get there, I cannot see and feel the beauty and calm. If I went to the beach, for example, for a time, I am physically there, but mentally I am distracted by anxiety, worry, and concerns back at home or work. I experience the sand, water, breeze, and ocean sounds, but I am not one with them. I am also not me, and I don't connect easily and intimately with others.

Over a few hours or days, as I let go of my mental/emotional juggling and let myself be in the moment, stillness and joy began to well up in me. Gradually, I became aware of myself and my surroundings in a refreshingly healthy way. It is then that I became the real me. My heart opens to the people with me, or possibly even to strangers I meet. I begin to enjoy strolling in complete oneness with my body and with the environment. When I hold the hand of my child, I am one with him. It have left the Mind Way and found fulfillment on the Soul Way.

—Have you, the reader, had a similar experience of the Soul Way?

Athletics: Athletes strive to be in what many call "the Zone," which is another term for the Soul Way. To get there, they stop mentally worrying, calculating, and planning. Instead, they let their soul-knowing guide them. When that happens, they become in the moment, one with the past and future—so much so that some athletes say that often they can tell what will happen next. They perform effortlessly with their bodies while watching the event unfold.

Coaches have noticed that when an entire team is in the Zone, they become almost unbeatable. The team members are no longer individuals, and instead, have become one soul, guided by a single source of inspiration. They react as one and flow effortlessly together to perform at their best.

Many leaders in industry, athletics, or the home understand the power of the Soul Way to live. They strive to create an environment where people make their soul-inspiration primary and use their mind-reasoning to check and guide their soul-insights. When people can do that, whether in a small or large group, they solve problems efficiently and joyfully.

—HAVE YOU EVER LIVED A SIMILAR SOUL WAY WHEN ATHLETIC?

Creating and Inventing: Creative people know that when they become still in the moment, when they make their calculating mind secondary to their soul-knowing, and when they suspend all their beliefs about the current project and become open to entirely new ways of seeing a situation, they connect with what some call "universal intelligence." Ideas seem to flow through them. They access insights not with their mind but with their soul intuition. As a result, inventions and art unfold naturally, bit by bit, all on their own. They watch as their soul guides their hands, body, and mind choreographically to produce wonders.

Some artists, such as jazz players and actors, notice that there can be times when they work together as one on the Soul Way. At those times, they connect to a common Source of inspiration that enables them to be organized and spontaneous at the same time. When in that soul-space, an actor might miss a line, and the entire troupe easily compensates. In a jazz band, one member may suddenly be inspired to do something completely unrehearsed, and members flow with his playing and enhance it. Together they watch as the music seems to flow through them in unity.

—Have you ever alone or in a group experienced the Soul Way when creating?

Mystical Experiences: I studied to be a priest in the Society of Jesus (Jesuits). There, I learned about fostering mystical experiences. They were not new to me because I had had many when I was younger, but I called them "oneness experiences." In them, I sensed the presence of Jesus; however, in conversations with others, I found that in their mystical experiences, they experienced what they called "God," "Spirit," or "my higher self."

When I was nineteen-years-old, I attended my first eight-day silent retreat at John Carroll University. In the first lecture that we attended, the priest leader invited us to go alone to someplace beautiful on campus and to ask ourselves the following question: "If you had to choose, would you want your soul or all of the comforts and material things that the world offers."

I did not understand the question; however, I decided for the first time to reflect on my future life. So, I climbed up the steps to the top floor of the administration building, found an empty room with a window overlooking Cleveland, and asked the question. After some time, I was transported into the most profound oneness experience. Time became eternal. I was living in the past, in the now, and in the future. Then, I became one with my soul, and the answer to the priest's question became obvious: I wanted to be my soul and one with all forever. I would give up the world to live like that.

For two days, I remained in that experience, sometimes walking with Jesus who seemed to be present by my side.

By the end of the retreat, I had decided to devote myself to him and to helping others. So, a year later, I entered the Jesuit seminary to study to be a priest.

But then, problems arose. Outside the seminary, I had many oneness experiences that provided the insights I needed to grow personally. However, in the seminary, I was taught to conform to Catholic and Jesuit rules and beliefs. When my independent insights contradicted those parameters, my "spiritual director" told me that I was "listening to the evil one," and not Spirit.

Over time, I became conflicted inside and between me and my superiors. I could not find a way to be faithful to my soul voice and the voices of religious authorities. I did not know it then, but I was struggling to live both on the Soul Way and the Mind Way. So finally, with great sorrow, I left the Jesuits and religion, while maintaining my commitment to Jesus and living, what I now call, "The Soul Way."

In the Jesuits, we had access to a large spiritual library. In many books, I discovered that mystics had described the differences between the Soul Way and the Mind Way in insightful ways. Some examples:

THE MIND WAY AND THE DARK EXPERIENCE	THE SOUL WAY AND THE LIGHT EXPERIENCE
I was born, I exist, I will die.	I am eternal.
There is divine, human, animal, and plant life.	Everything, including a rock, is a unique version of the same intelligent life at various levels of evolution.
Everything happens through luck and coincidence, except when God intervenes.	Everything is ordered to provide what we most deeply and often unconsciously desire.
I am alone with my thoughts.	Everyone and everything speaks to me when I listen with my soul.
I am sometimes loved.	I am one with love and with my Source of inspiration.

—HAVE YOU HAD A MYSTICAL EXPERIENCE? HOW WOULD YOU DESCRIBE IT?

Transition

As you have read above, people describe the differences between the Mind and Soul Ways sometimes similarly, and sometimes with unique insights. As we study the words of Eve, Abraham, Buddha, and Jesus, we will see that they also described the two Ways sometimes with the same words and metaphors that you read above, and sometimes with terminology of their own invention. In any case, I think you will discover that their mission was to teach us how to leave the Mind Way to find our fulfillment on the Soul Way.

Buddha and the Two Ways to Live

Ancient wise people such as Eve, Abraham, Buddha, and Jesus did not distinguish between emotional and spiritual health. They observed that both happened together. They also noted the vast difference between the Mind Way and the Soul Way. They regarded the latter as the method for personal development. Therefore, as observational therapists, not abstract theologians or philosophers, they taught people how to live practically to achieve both mental and spiritual health.

Throughout the book, we will quote extensively from their works. When we do so, you will read a two-column format. On the left is my translation of the original text. On the right is a rephrasing that explains what I consider to be the meaning of the metaphors in the text. There follows one of Buddha's poems in *The Dhammapada* (Ch. 26) in which he refers to both Ways.

Few
cross the river
of desires, passions, and
hatred.[1]

[1]*Few cross the river of desires, passions, and hatred:* Few people use the Soul Way to conquer the upsetting emotions of the Dark Experience.

Most
stay on this side
of the river
running up and down.[2]

[2]*Most stay on this side of the river, running up and down:* Most remain on the Mind Way, running from one distraction to another so that they will not notice their dark emotional pain.

But
the wise man,
on the Way
crosses over
beyond death.[3]

[3]*But the wise man on the Way crosses over beyond death.* But the wise person following the Soul Way conquers the emotional death in the Dark Experience.

He
abandons the Dark Way
for the Light Way,[4]

[4]*He abandons the Dark Way for the Light Way:* He leaves The Mind Way for the Soul Way.

And
celebrating his freedom,
the wise man
becomes a light
pure, brilliant, and free.[5]

[5]*And celebrating his freedom, the wise man becomes a light.* And celebrating his freedom from the Mind Way, the wise person becomes free to be the light to people enslaved in the dark world.

METAPHORS

You, the reader, may be asking, "How do you know what the metaphors in this poem mean? For example, "In the above poem, how do you know that 'this side' is the Mind Way?"

My editors and I determine the meaning of a metaphor in several ways. First, we look at the organization of the text as we determined it to be using Semitic Parallelism principles.[2] That method usually shows us that an author will place his definition of a metaphor in a parallel passage. Secondly, we study how the author uses a metaphor throughout his work. Thirdly, we research how other ancient authors have used the metaphor. And finally, we reflect on ourselves and decide how we live the metaphor on the two ways. Then, we offer you, the reader, our *opinions*.

---

[2] Semitic Parallelism

There is no official dictionary of ancient wisdom metaphors. People often disagree about their meaning, especially when they do not understand that in the Bible, the authors often describe the Soul Way, which is opposite the Mind Way taught in religions.

To help you, we offer you the results of our research. We may do that in a way that reads as if we know the absolute truth. That is not the case, nor is it our intent. We could continuously repeat the phrase, "in our opinion," but that would get boring. So, while the wording we have chosen may come across as factual or absolute, ultimately, you must decide the meaning of a metaphor for yourself.

BUDDHA'S TWO WAY POEM

In the above poem, Buddha observes the two Ways to live and then describes them. In doing so, he establishes a two-part practical goal for personal development: to be free from painful emotions and to be a brilliant, free light to others.

We also notice that Buddha does not say that there are more than two ways to live, nor that one can be on both ways at the same time. They are mutually exclusive. We can choose to be on one way or the other way, but only if we take the time, as he did, to become aware of them, to describe them in detail to ourselves, and to master the discipline of being on the Soul Way.

Jesus and the Two Ways to Live

Buddha called the Dark Experience a type of psychological "death." Jesus, in *The Gospel of Thomas* (Saying 56) likewise calls the Dark Experience, a "world" of "death."

<table>
<tr>
<td>

Whoever
has known the world
has discovered a corpse.[1]

And
whoever
has discovered a corpse[2]

The world
is
worthy
of him
not.[3]

</td>
<td>

[1]*Whoever has known the world has discovered a corpse.* Whoever sees normal people in the world today has discovered a walking, living death.

[2]*And whoever has discovered a corpse:* And whoever recognizes that most people are living psychological/ spiritual death...

[3]*The world is worthy of him not:* Those dead are not worthy of the presence of those alive.

</td>
</tr>
</table>

The last stanza is a very strong statement; however, Jesus was a warrior. He intended to die trying to save us from what most consider healthy.

In this poem, Jesus says that the first step to becoming fulfilled is to "discover" living dark, death (a "corpse") in ourselves and the people around us. When we have done that, we know, first, that that is not how we want to live, and second, that we need to find a radically different way to find fulfillment.

The Foundational Question

Wise people, like Eve, Abraham, Buddha, and Jesus, discovered the differences between the Mind and Soul Ways. So, we are led to ask, "Why does not everyone do that?" Jesus answers that question when he defines both the Soul Way and the Light Experience as a "Kingdom" in *the Gospel of Thomas,* (Saying 3):

The Kingdom,[1]

It
is
of your eye[2]
inward,[3]

And
it
is
of your eye
outward.[4]

[1] *The Kingdom:* A way of being in which a person lives on the Soul Way to be in the Light.

[2] *Eye:* One's third-eye. On the Soul Way, one uses a single *intuitive* eye to understand oneself and life.

[3] *It is of your eye inward:* In the Kingdom, you intuitively know yourself differently.

[4] *It is of your eye outward:* In the Kingdom, you intuitively know everyone and everything outside of you differently.

For Jesus, the "Kingdom" is not something spiritual. A person knows when he is in the Kingdom because his perceptions of himself and others undergo a major shift. As a result, he transforms his emotions, thoughts, and actions.

We introduced this poem with the question: "Why does not everyone discover the difference between the Soul and Mind Ways?

Jesus's answer: Because most people do not master knowing themselves and the world around them with their third, intuitive-eye. Instead, they *primarily* understand themselves, others, and the nature of the universe with their two eyes, which is a metaphor for their rational reasoning and beliefs.

Mental vs. Intuitive Knowing

The Mind Way	The Soul Way
Two-eyed knowing	One-eyed knowing
Uses reason primarily	Use intuition primarily
Logically arrives at his beliefs	Immediately knows

Many cultures recognize that mastering our "third-eye" is the key to personal development. They show that by putting a dot on their forehead or by wearing something signifying the third-eye.

For thousands of years, people have recognized that our "single-eyed" soul-knowing is the powerful, intuitive way to obtain information to live life fully. We can't live on the Soul Way by using primarily our two-eyed mental reasoning. That is why you will read that Eve, Abraham, Buddha, and Jesus taught us how to develop our intuitive knowing.

Summary

At any moment, we only can be on one of two Ways: The Mind Way that leads us deeper into the Dark Experience, or the Soul Way that guides us into the Light Experience.

We primarily get insights with our third-eye intuition on the Soul Way. With that faculty, we understand and live life at a higher level.

In the pyramid below, we see our third, intuitive eye placed at the top. It represents how the wise primarily view everything. The up-arrow in the chart signifies our evolution from the Dark Way to the Light Way:

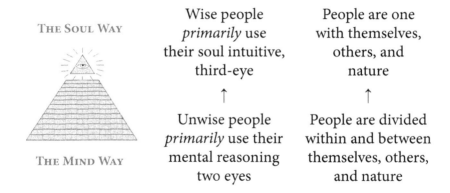

THE SOUL WAY		Wise people *primarily* use their soul intuitive, third-eye	People are one with themselves, others, and nature
		↑	↑
THE MIND WAY		Unwise people *primarily* use their mental reasoning two eyes	People are divided within and between themselves, others, and nature

Forever, people have been aware of the radical difference between the Mind Way and the Soul Way. A sample of what wise people called them is below:

PERSON	DATE	CALLED THE MIND WAY AND THE DARK EXPERIENCE	CALLED THE SOUL WAY AND THE LIGHT EXPERIENCE
Eve	-500 BCE[3]	Nod (State of wandering)	Garden of Eden
Abraham	-500 BCE	Foreign Land	Promised Land
Buddha	483/400 BCE	The World, Death, Slavery, Darkness	Nirvana,[4] Life, Freedom, Light
Jesus	4 BCE – 30 CE	The World, Death, Darkness, Poverty, Division	The Kingdom, Life, Light, Richness, Oneness
Buber	1878-1956	I-It Relationship	I-Thou Relationship
Maslow	1908-1970	The Normal Experience	A Plateau of Peak Experiences
Artists Athletes	Today	Difficult, Intricate, Labored	The Zone, Easy, Flowing
Mystics	Today	Mundane, Dry, Divided, Alone, Transient	Mystical, Enlightened, One, Bathed in Love, Eternal

---

[3] BCE: Before the Common Era. This is preferred by scholars now rather than "BC."

[4] *Nirvana*: Buddha never used that term. Later followers described the Light Experience that way.

An Exercise to Prepare for the Next Chapters:

To live the Soul Way, one must become acutely aware of the pain of being in the Dark Experience and the joy of being in the Light Experience. Then, when in the Dark, one can use the Soul Way to evolve into Light.

I offer the following suggestions for practicing what those on the Soul Way do continually: to notice the difference between the Light and Dark Experience.

1. Go to a place that is beautiful and quiet. Pay attention to the beauty around you until your mind and emotions become still.

2. Recall when you most intensely experienced a Light Experience. Perhaps it was when you held your new-born child for the first time, or when you walked alone on the beach, or when a drug took you to another world. Describe your intense Light Experience to yourself. How did you perceive things around you? How did you view yourself? Were you mentally in the past, present, or future? What were you feeling? What was different about your thinking?

3. Recall when you most intensely experienced a Dark Experience Perhaps when you were very upset. Describe that Experience to yourself. How did you perceive things around you? How did you view yourself? Were you mentally in the past, present, or future? What were you feeling? What was different about your thinking? Did you know how to evolve into a Light Experience?

CHAPTER TWO

THE GARDEN OF EDEN ALLEGORY: OUR BIRTH

Introduction

Eve noticed the difference between the Dark and the Light Experience. She used her soul-intuition to determine how to be on the Soul Way all day, every day in an ever more profound manner. She then, imbedded her insights in the Garden of Eden story.

The Garden narrative features a "Tree of the Knowledge of Life." Because we have never seen such a tree, we know that it is a metaphor for a way to know things. That tells us that we are reading an allegory. It is *not* a historical account of something that happened a long time ago.

Archaeologists have found symbols of the Tree of the Knowledge of Life carved and painted in stone, clay, wood, and fabric on every continent.

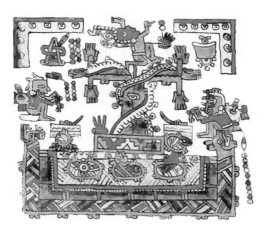

South American Olmec Tree of Life

The Olmec society lasted from about 1600 BCE to around 350 BCE. That means that they knew of the Garden Allegory long before the Spaniards arrived in 1492 CE.

Buddha (c. 563/480 – c. 483/400 BCE) over in North India probably knew the Garden Allegory. We suspect he did because he "sat under" (metaphorically, "lived with") the Bodhi Tree (a tree of enlightenment) to become wise. That was probably a term used for the Tree of the Knowledge of Life

TYPES OF ALLEGORIES

An allegory is a narrative about one or more principal characters. The story consists of symbolic figures, actions, imagery, and events, which together create the moral, spiritual, or political meaning that the author wishes to convey.

An example is Homer's extended epic poem, *The Odyssey*. That work focuses on the Greek hero Odysseus, king of Ithaca, and his journey home after the fall of Troy. It is based loosely on historical events, which Homer changes to suit his primary purpose: to show how Odysseus both develops and declines in character as he encounters problems. As Homer does that, he teaches us how we might do the same in analogous situations.

In *The Odyssey*, as in most allegories, all the characters represent each of us in some way. Further, the animals and things in the story symbolize or are metaphors for aspects of ourselves. However, because Homer includes some facts that historians know happened, he composed a historical allegory, part history, part allegory.

In the Bible, we find some "pure allegories" with no historical facts. The Garden of Eden book in Genesis is an example. There are a few verses that tell of the physical location of the Garden; however, in my Book, *The Semitic Secret*, the structure of the text shows that a copyist inserted the description of the rivers around the Garden (Gen 2:10-14) after the original was composed. Otherwise, there are no historical facts in the narrative.

In both pure allegories and historical allegories, the author intends *primarily* to show character development or decline, not history. Consequently, in a historical allegory he may distort historical facts and invent things that never happened. That presents problems for historians and archaeologists when they try to research whether biblical events occurred, and conundrums for people who seek absolute truth in the *Bible*.

The Garden Allegory

The *Garden of Eden Allegory:* is the second story in the *Bible*.[5] Eve first tells us about the birth of a person (Genesis 2:6-7):

(Being-Gods
commanded:)

And
there
went up a mist
from the land

And
it
watered the whole face
of the earth.

And
Being-Gods
formed a person
of dust
of the earth

And
breathed into his nostrils
the breath
of life;

And
the person
became a living being.

---

[5] Robert W. North, *The Garden of Eden Allegory: in Its Original Poetic Organization,* 2018.

Parentheses

(Being-Gods commanded): I discovered what I call "Semitic Parallelism"—how many Semitic authors organized their works. In my book, *The Semitic Secret,* I show how the organization tells us when texts have been inserted or deleted from the original by later copyists. I show these insertions or deletions by putting them in parenthesis. In this case, something like the phrase "Being-Gods commanded" was deleted. By using techniques that I explain in *The Semitic Secret,* we can approximate the original text.

Back to the Allegory

Being-Gods: The words "Being-Gods" are my translation of the Hebrew "Yĕhovah "Elohiym," which is what Eve calls "God" in the Garden Allegory. "Yĕhovah" can be rendered as "Being." "Elohiym" is plural, and it means "Gods."

The Bible begins with the sentence, "In the beginning, 'Elohiym (the Gods) created heaven and earth." It is common to believe that the Hebrews believe that God is "one." *That is not true.* Many experienced multiple Gods. In most current translations of the Bible, "Yĕhovah 'Elohiym" is rendered as "the Lord God," which is not only inaccurate but makes the text almost impossible to understand as the author intended.

Jesus and Two Gods in One

Like the early Hebrews, Jesus tells us in *The Gospel of Thomas* that he experienced two persons in one God. He calls them, "Father" and "Mother" as we read in the following poem (Saying 105):

He

Who
will know the Father
and
the Mother,[1]

[1]*He who will know the Father and the Mother:* Anyone who will experience God as both a Father and as a Mother...

He
will be referred to
as
the son
of a harlot.[2]

[2]*He will be referred to as the son of a harlot.* He will be called the son (or daughter) of an evil woman.

In this poem, Jesus speaks of two-parent Gods as joined in oneness in the birth process. He also tells us that one does not "know" them through blind faith, but instead through direct experience. Those who either hold that God is "one" or who believe that one cannot directly experience two Gods in a oneness may call a person making such claims the son of an evil mother (as we read in the last stanza above).

What are We Going to Call "God?"

What are we going to call "God" in this book? People have suggested to me: "Source," "Higher Self," "Father," "Parents," "Spirit," and of course, by many other names, such as "Allah," "Yĕhovah," "Elohiym," and "Brahma."

After a great deal of reflection and after talking to many people, I was led to call God in this book, "Spirit." This term seems to fit most traditions. You, the reader, may call God whatever you want, of course.

BACK TO THE ALLEGORY

Being-Gods commanded. Often, in an allegory, when Spirit commands, we are to understand that God is not talking directly to people. Instead, the command is a natural law. Often it is one that is part of our nature. In that case, we know it unconsciously. Authors, such as Eve, stop and make conscious the directive within them that people do not notice.

For example, a mother unconsciously knows a command to protect and nurture her child. To express that notion explicitly, an author might say, "Being-Gods commanded the woman to nurture and guard her child."

Being-Gods commanded: Within us is a natural directive.

Being-Gods commanded, and there went up a mist from the <u>land</u>, and it watered the whole face of the <u>earth</u>.

In Genesis, there are two words for what we call "ground." One is "erets," which I translate as "land." The other is "adama," which I render as "earth." There are *essential* differences in biblical metaphorical meaning between these two words.

We can understand how the Hebrews understood these two metaphors by studying their use in Jesus' *Parable of the Sower*. The following is *The Gospel of Thomas* version (Saying 9), which does not differ much from the other versions in the New Testament Gospels.

<table>
<tr><td>Behold![1]</td><td>[1]Behold: Third-eye see with your intuition!</td></tr>
<tr><td>He
went out</td><td></td></tr>
<tr><td>Namely
he</td><td>[2]He went out, the one who sows. A person who speaks in oneness with Spirit became present to another person.</td></tr>
<tr><td>The one
who
sows.[2]</td><td></td></tr>
</table>

And
he
filled his hand[3]
(with seed)

[3]*And filled his hand with seed:* A "hand" is one's ability to control. A "seed" is wisdom. Thus, the sower selects some wisdom carefully.

And
he
threw them.[4]

[4]*And he threw them:* And he confronted one or more people with words (seeds) of wisdom.

And
some
were
indeed
discovered
on the Way.[5]

[5]*And some were discovered on the way:* And some seeds of wisdom were heard by a person on the highly traveled Mind Way ("land").

And
they
came
Namely
the birds[6]

[6]*And they came, namely the birds:* Mental beliefs (birds) that were already in the listener's mind came forth.

And
they
gathered them.[7]

[7]*And they gathered them:* The listener made his old beliefs more important than the new wisdom.

And
some others
indeed
were discovered
on rock.[8]

[8]*Some others were discovered on a rock.* Some seeds of wisdom were heard by a closed, stubborn mind.

And
they
did
not send roots
down to the earth[9]

[9]*They did not send roots down to the earth:* The seeds of wisdom did not enter into the receptive, reflective consciousness of the listener.

And
they
did
not send ears
rising to heaven.[10]

[10]*And they did not send ears rising to heaven:* The seeds of wisdom did not produce higher level understandings.

And
some others
indeed
were discovered
in thorns[11]

And
they
choked the descendant[12]

And
the worm
ate them.[13]

And
some others
were discovered
in the earth[14]

Which
was
good to them[15]

And
they
gave fruit
up to heaven[16]

Which
was
good to it.[17]

And
it
came
Some
60 per measure
And some
120 per measure.[18]

[11]*And some were discovered in thorns:* And some seeds of wisdom were heard by a person with attachments (thorns) to beliefs, people, and things. Thorns grow on land, that is, on unreceptive, unreflective, consciousness (the Mind Way).

[12]*And they chocked the seeds:* And the person made his attachments to people and things more important than wisdom.

[13]*And the worm ate them:* And the person let his worry about the people and things to which he is attached become more important than the wisdom.

[14]*And some others were discovered in the earth:* And some other seeds of wisdom entered into the person's receptive, reflective consciousness.

[15]*Which was good to them:* Which nourished them.

[16]*And they gave fruit up to heaven:* And the wisdom enabled the person to live a higher level of life.

[17]*Which was good to it:* The "it" is "earth." The higher we live, the more fertile our earth (receptive, reflective consciousness).

[18]*60 per measure – 120 per measure:* Some wise insights generated more of a fulfilled life than others.

This parable by Jesus is about each of us. We receive inspiration continually. We only hear those ideas and integrate them when we put them in our "earth" (our receptive, reflective consciousness). We do that on the Soul Way.

We are fertile earth when we are open to being upset by new, inspired ideas. They often confront us with our limitations and faults and show us how we can evolve to higher levels of fulfilled living.

When we are "land," we are unreceptive, unreflective consciousness on the Mind Way. We are not unconscious, but semi-conscious, living out automatically our former beliefs and habits.

In the parable, we are "land" when we are the hard, traveled way, that is, when we automatically think the ideas given to us from society. We are also "land" when we are closed-minded, that is when we are a "rock." And finally, we are "land" when we are "thorns," that is when we are attached to beliefs, people, and things. In those ways, we make other people and things more important than growing in wisdom.

BACK TO THE ALLEGORY

There went up a mist from the land, and it watered the whole face of the earth.

"To water" in the Bible is "to inspire." A "mist," then, are tiny seeds of inspiration. The mist rises from our inner semi-conscious "land" when we pay attention to it. We then plant the inspired seeds in our consciousness ("earth") where we can reflect on them and use them to change our lives.

A "face" is one's unique manifestation of one's soul. As we become more conscious, our face changes.

There went up a mist from the land, and it watered the whole face of the earth. Wisdom rose from our unreflective semi-consciousness, and it inspired our entire reflective consciousness.

Being-Gods formed a person of the dust of the earth and breathed into his nostrils the breath of life.

Being Gods formed a person: The Hebrew word here for "person" is "'adam." It can mean "person," a "human being," "mankind," or "man." Many translations read: "Being-Gods formed Adam." But "'adam" is *not* a proper name. *No one in the allegory is named "Adam,"* nor do we know at this point in the allegory whether the person is a man or woman.

(In my book, *The Semitic Secret,* I present the evidence that the one instance of the name "Eve" in the Allegory was not in the original composition. *Thus, there is no one named either Adam or Eve in the Allegory.*)

Being-Gods formed a person of the dust of the earth: "Dust" is a tiny bit of receptive, reflective consciousness.

Being-Gods breathed into his nostrils: A "face" is the presentation of one's unique self to the world. In the center of one's face is one's "nostrils." Metaphorically, the spirit of a person enters and exits through the nostrils. For example, when one's nostrils flare, the air rushes in and out in anger. When one is peaceful, the air enters and exits slowly and peacefully. One's face changes depending on the nature of the spirit that enters or exits our nostrils.

Being-Gods…breathed into his nostrils the breath of life: Spirit took some divine life and made the person come alive as a son or daughter. Thus, Eve tells us that she observed that at our core, we are *divine.* She maintains that there are *not* two kinds of life, divine life and human life. Each of us possesses a "face," that is, a unique, soul version of the same divine life.

Being-Gods formed a person of the dust of the earth and breathed into his nostrils the breath of life.

The historical interpretation: Spirit made the first person on earth of reflective consciousness and then, gave him human life.

The first-level allegorical meaning: Every child is born with receptive, reflective consciousness, and divine life.

The second-level allegorical meaning: In each moment, each of us may choose to become more reflectively conscious of our soul's divine life.

JESUS VS. CHRISTIAN THEOLOGY

Christianity distinguishes divine life from human life. In contrast, Jesus observed that we each at the soul level are divine. He says that in the following poem from *The Gospel of Thomas* (Saying 3b):

When you should know yourselves,[1]	[1]*When you should know yourselves:* When you should know the real you…
Then they will know you[2]	[2]*Then, they will know you:* Then, people will see a radical difference in you.
And you will realize[3]	[3]*And you will realize:* And you will possess external confirmation.
That you are sons of the Father Who lives.[4]	[4]*That you are sons of the Father, who lives:* That you are divine sons and daughters of Spirit who lives in you.

In this poem, Jesus does *not* say that he is *not* the son of Spirit (God). Instead, he says that we are *all* born as sons and daughters of Spirit. We know that when we know ourselves.

EXERCISE:

QUESTIONS FOR REFLECTION:

1. When you, the reader, embrace a new-born child, do you sense that you are holding a human being with a core-life different from divine life or a person with a unique version of divine life?

2. Recall that there are two ways to live: in the Dark Experience on the Way of the Mind and in the Light Experience on the Way of the Soul. Eve and Jesus looked carefully at a child and saw divine life. That presents a problem: How could we who were born with divine life possess a Dark Experience?

MY ANSWERS:

1. When you, the reader, embrace a new-born child, do you sense that you are holding a human with a core-life different from divine life, or a person with a unique version divine life? **My answer:** When I am alive and enlightened in the Light Experience, I experience divine life in everyone and everything.

2. Recall that there are two ways to live: in the Dark Experience on the Way of the Mind and in the Light Experience on the Way of the Soul. Eve and Jesus looked carefully at a child and saw divine life. That presents a problem. How could we who were born with divine life possess a Dark Experience? We will read Jesus' answer to that question in *The Gospel of Thomas* (Saying 24):

The Light
exists inward
of a man
of light[1]

And
he
comes to be light
to the world,[2]

[1] *The Light exists inward of a man of light:* The divine light exists in a person.

[2] *And he comes to be light to the world:* A divine light-infused person comes to be the light guide for those on the Way of the Mind in the Dark's Experience.

All
of it.[3]

[3]*All of it:* When a person presents divine life to others, he manifests not a likeness of Spirit, but complete divine life. E.g., When we see the light in a child, we see God.

If
he
does
not come to be light,[4]

[4]*When he does not come to be light:* When a person chooses not to be the light that he is in his soul...

The darkness
is
he."[5]

[5]*If he does not come to be light, the darkness is he:* If a person does not live out the divine life that he is at his core, he chooses to be a dark false self on the Mind Way.

In this poem, Jesus uses the terms "light" and "darkness" to describe two ways to be in the world.

The question we are asking: "How can a person who is divine light become darkness?" In this poem, Jesus' answer is this: To the degree that we do not live who we essentially are, to that degree, we live a false life. *Thus, to be fully alive in the Garden (Light) Experience, we need to be who we are.*

Jesus, unlike most Christian theologians and clergy, does not say that to be full of light, one needs to embrace Christian doctrine or any other religious system. For Jesus, a person is born "saved," "whole," "perfect," and "sinless." He does not need a baptism cleansing of original sin. To be fulfilled in the Garden, he only needs to stop being false and return to his birth state. (Eve will explain later how we do that).

Buddha and Being Yourself

Throughout the book, I want to show that Jesus and Buddha usually agree when they teach how to live the Soul Way. Jesus has said that to be what we are, divine life, we need to know ourselves. Below, Buddha (Ch. 2) says the same thing with his metaphors:

The master
watches[1]

[1]*The master watches:* An evolved, light person observes his every thought and emotion to know himself (this is what Jesus said).

And
he
is clear.[2]

[2]*He is clear:* He is singly himself and not false.

How joyful
he
is[3]

[3]*How joyful he is:* How joyful he is to be himself and not false.

For
he
knows that wakefulness
is
life.[4]

[4]*He knows that wakefulness is life:* He understands that one must be fully conscious of who he is to live in the Light Experience.

So wake up,
reflect,
watch.[5]

[5]*So wake up, reflect, watch:* So know yourself.

Work with diligence
and
attention.[6]

[6]*Work with diligence and attention:* Confront your falseness and live your real self.

Live on the Way
And
the light
will develop in you.[7]

[7]*Live on the Way, and the light will develop in you:* Live on the Soul Way, and you will become the light that you are.

Like Jesus, Buddha taught us that to grow in light, we need to know ourselves. In that way, we can choose to be who we are. A person who does not know himself will wander through life in darkness, that is, by being a false self.

The Garden Allegory continues with further descriptions of who we are (Gen 2:15):

> *Being-Gods*
> *took the person*
>
> *And*
> *put that one*
> *into the Garden*
> *of Eden*
> *to nourish it*
> *and*
> *to guard it.*

Being-Gods took the person and put that one into the Garden of Eden ("Eden" means "Pleasure").

The historical interpretation: Spirit chose ("took") the first person on earth and birthed him ("put that one") into a physical Garden of Pleasure.

The general allegorical meaning: Every child is born in the Garden of Pleasure (in the Light Experience).

The practical, personal allegorical meaning: At any time, each of us may use Spirit inspiration to take ourselves out of the Dark Experience and put us in the Light Experience.

Being-Gods took the person and put that one into the Garden of Eden *to nourish it* and *to guard it*. Our job for the rest of our lives is to "nourish" the Garden Experience (the Light Experience) and to "guard" it.

EXERCISE:

QUESTIONS FOR REFLECTION:

1. How do you "nourish" your Garden (Soul) Experience?

2. How do you "guard" your Garden Experience?

MY ANSWERS:

1. "How do you "nourish" your Garden Experience?" **My answer:**

   a. I study my past Garden experiences. For example, I examine my life and identify those times:
      i. When I was completely fulfilled without a single worry or regret,
      ii. When I was still, living in the moment and not mentally in the past or future,
      iii. When I was one with myself, others and my environment,
      iv. When I was thinking and acting with confidence and ease.
      v. When I was full of unconditional love for myself and others.
   b. I study how I created my past Garden Experiences.
   c. I ask Spirit to show me what I do to keep myself in the Dark Experience instead of putting myself in the Garden Experience.
   d. I plan on how to make changes in my life to live more in the Garden.

2. "How do you "guard" your Garden Experience?" **My answer:**

   a. I limit involvement with people who are on the Mind Way.
   b. I decide to make being in the Garden more important than being in the Dark Experience.
   c. I seek out others who make the Garden Experience important and learn from them how they do it.

Eve tells us that we were emotionally healthy in the Garden of Eden when we were born because we were truly ourselves. We left it because we did not possess the wisdom to guard ourselves against adults who taught us to be false. Our remembrance of the Garden motivates us to get back into it and live there all day, every day. Therefore, our model for what we seek is the light, real child, not the dark, false adult.

OUR GOAL ACCORDING TO JESUS

In many of Jesus' parables, he taught us that we could be fully evolved and fulfilled if we would return to being a little child. Here is an example from the Gospel of Thomas (Saying 4):

He
will delay
not[1]

[1]*He will delay not:* The wise person will not delay seeking to live 24/7 in the Garden.

Namely
the man
of maturity
in his days[2]

[2]*The man of maturity in his days:* The word "day" means a time of enlightenment. So, a "man of maturity" is an enlightened person.

To ask a little
small child,[3]

[3]*To ask a small little child:* The wise person humbles himself to experience Garden life in a tiny child. He wants the child to teach him to be real.

He
being
of seven days,[4]

[4]*He being of seven days:* Biblically, the number seven means "perfection." A child is born with perfect divine life and light.

About the place
of life[5]

[5]*About the place of life:* The wise person seeks to be one with the center of life in a child because that is where he is also one with himself and others.

And
he
will live.[6]

[6]*And he will live:* And he will become more his core divine life.

A child lives from his "place" of divine "life." In contrast, dark adults live from their dead, false-self center, which some call the "ego." The more we live from there, the more we suffer emotionally in the Dark Experience.

According to Eve, we die when we become what we are not. We live when we are congruent with our soul's divine life. By extension, a person in soul-oneness with himself is automatically in soul-oneness with everyone else, because everyone is a unique version of the divine soul.

We die when, unlike a child, we maintain that we are important (holy, valuable, and successful) because of our religious faith, money, things, race, nationality, appearance, title, reputation, traditions, politics, etc. We live in the light in the Garden when we identify only with who we are.

As an example, Hitler's soul essence was divine life. He chose to divide himself mentally from that experience and live many false selves when he identified with being a German national, a powerful leader, his race, his politics, etc. When he took on those false identifications, he automatically disconnected from himself and others. It was that lack of being one with others that enabled him to torture and kill without feeling their pain.

Jesus sums up the difference between the life in an adult-child and that in an adult-adult in *The Gospel of Thomas* (Saying 28):

I stood on my feet[1] in the midst of the world[2]	[1]*I stood on my feet:* Presented myself fully and strongly as a tiny child.
	[2]*In the midst of the world:* In the midst of adults who do not live the life of a little child.
And I appeared to them in the flesh[3]	[3]*I appeared to them in the flesh:* I demonstrated tangibly to them how an adult could live from the center of life like a little child.
And I discovered them, All of them, drunk;[4]	[4]*Drunk:* Dark and deluded
For blind men[5]	[5]*Blind men:* Men who cannot use their intuition to see divine life in a little child.

They
are in their heart[6]

And
they
peer inward
and outward
not;[7]

For
they
have come into the
world
empty

And
they
also
seek to go out
of the world
empty.[8]

[6]*In their heart:* In their intuitive love center.

[7]*They peer inward and outward not:* They do not soul-observe the true nature of themselves and others.

[8]*They have come into the world empty, and they seek to go out of the world empty:* They were born as their real selves and "empty" of false selves, and they seek to die full of false selves and empty of their real selves.

Buddha's Model

Like Jesus, Buddha also tells us the importance of selecting the right model for what we hope to become in the following poem (Ch. 5):

If
the traveler[1]
cannot find a master[2]
to accompany him

He
should travel alone
rather than
with a fool[3]
for a partner.

[1]*Traveler:* A person seeking to go deeper into the Light Experience

[2]*Master:* A person who has lost his ego (a collection of false selves) and who has become a tiny child again.

[3]*Fool:* An adult who is full of false selves on the Mind Way.

Summary

THE SOUL WAY

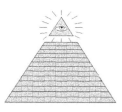

THE MIND WAY

A wise person becomes a little child again in the Garden with the wisdom to guard himself against those who want him not to be his divine self.

↑

An Unwise person lives in the Dark Experience because he chooses to be his ego.

CHAPTER THREE

THE GARDEN OF EDEN ALLEGORY: THE GARDEN COMMAND

INTRODUCTION

Eve holds that we are born fulfilled in the Garden. She then tells us that we need to "nourish" and "guard" that Light experience. In this second part of the Allegory, she will explain that we do those two things by obeying a command that is deep in our being. Most of us are unaware that there is a natural law that tells us how to live on the Soul Way. She took the time to know herself and to articulate what we need to do and not do to get back into and remain in the Garden.

THE GARDEN COMMAND

Being-Gods
commanded the person:

"Of the (fruit)[6]
of the Tree
(of the Knowledge
of Life)
in the (middle of the) Garden of Eden[7]
take

---

[6] *Fruit:* Implied. See: Gen. 3:2

[7] Eve tells us the Tree of the Knowledge of Life is in the middle of the Garden in Gen. 2:9.

And

eat

And

eat;

Of the (fruit) of the Tree
of the Knowledge
of Good and Bad
do
not take

And

eat;

And

eat;

For
on the day
you
eat of it

You
will die

And
die."[8]

(Genesis 2:16-17)

Being-Gods commanded the person: The Garden Command is in our being. Spirit reveals it to everyone who seeks it. Often, in allegories, such commands are presented as if Spirit speaks to them from the clouds to us.

---

[8] This translation of the Garden Command includes a few words that we do not find in our current Hebrew texts. However, I show in my book, *The Semitic Secret*, that the original was what you see above.

Tree of the Knowledge of Life. Rooted in our being is a way to know "life." Two stanzas later, Eve tells us that we have another "tree," which is a way to know "good and bad." That is confusing. Eve, on the one hand, says that we have *two* trees or ways to know, and on the other, that we can know anything in *three* ways, as "good," "bad," and "life." So, let us examine Eve's logic.

When we know something as "good," we also know that that something could be "bad." Thus, to know good is to know bad and to know bad is to know good. So, that is *one* Tree (or way) of Knowing.

So now, we need to ask, "What is the opposite of knowing anyone or anything as bad and good?"

Exercise:

Eve says that we automatically know anyone or anything with two trees of knowledge: The Tree of the Knowledge of Good and Bad and the Tree of the Knowledge of Life.

Question for Reflection: When we know "life," what are we knowing? In other words, what is the opposite of knowing good and bad?

My answer: To know "life" is to know all as "perfect-as-is." This is a special way of knowing that some call "sublime knowing."

Exercise:

Eve tells us that we know all in two ways: As good-bad or as life (as perfect-as-is, or as sublime).

Questions for Reflection:

1. When you held a newborn baby, did you perceive that child as bad, good, perfect-as-is, full of life, or full of death?

2. When you sat beside the bed of a little sleeping one, did you perceive that child as bad, good, perfect-as-is, full of life, or full of death?

3. When you were in wonder at the beauty of a sunset, a song, or a piece of art, did you know it as bad, good, perfect-as-is, full of life, or full of death?

My answers:

1. When you held a newborn baby, did you perceive that child as bad, good, perfect-as-is, full of life, or full of death? **My answer:** Usually, whether it is a newborn child or animal, I am in awe of that little one. I see the sublime in him, and that he is full of life and perfect-as-is.

2. When you sat beside the bed of a little sleeping one, did you perceive that child as bad, good, perfect-as-is, full of life, or full of death? **My answer:** I remember the bad and good that he has done, but usually I make that knowing secondary to seeing him as perfect-as-is and full of life.

3. When you were in wonder at the beauty of a sunset, a song, or a piece of art, did you know it as bad, good, perfect-as-is, full of life, or full of death? **My answer:** I experience the sublime in those things—that they are perfect-as-is. In a type of mystical moment, I find them to be alive in a way that I cannot explain.

Back to the Allegory

Of the fruit of the Tree of the Knowledge of Life in the middle of the Garden of Eden take and eat and eat:

Fruit: Fruit is an *experience* that results from a way of knowing. As I explained in Chapter One, we live in at any moment in one of only two general kinds of experiences: the Dark Experience or the Light Experience.

Middle of the Garden: Core of the Garden (Light) Experience.

Take: To "take" is to choose.

Eat: To "eat" is to take in something, enjoy it, and make it part of us.

Of the fruit of the Tree of the Knowledge of Life in the middle of the Garden of Eden, take, and eat, and eat. As we "eat" (enjoy) the Garden Experience, we make it part of every cell in our body. As we do that, we become deeply fulfilled.

Of the fruit of the Tree of the Knowledge of Good or Bad, do not take and eat. Of the Dark Experience (fruit) of the Tree that is not at the core of who you are, do not eat (enjoy it).

For on the day that you eat of it, you will die and die. For in the moment of free choice when you choose to enjoy the Dark Experience, you will live a type of spiritual and psychological death.

We know we have "died" when we live in the past or future. We also experience a roller coaster emotional life—from sadness to happiness, from regret to worry, from depression to out-of-body excitement, on and on. (Remember from Chapter One how Maslow, Buber, Buddha, Jesus and others described the Dark Experience).

Eve's Grand Insight

The Garden Command tells us that we *automatically* know anyone or anything with *both* Trees. We cannot stop ourselves from knowing bad and good. In other words, we automatically know All as perfect-as-is at the same time that we know All as bad and good.

While we automatically know with both trees at the same time, we can *choose* which "fruit" (experience) to "eat" (enjoy). The more we eat the Garden Experience, the more we become light in the dark world.

That is Eve's grand insight. We cannot choose our knowing, but we can decide which "fruit" (experience) to enjoy.

Eve's Theory of Personal Evolution or Devolution

We Automatically	As a Result We Automatically	We Decide Consciously or Unconsciously	As a Result We Automatically
Know with the Tree of the Knowledge of Life and with the Tree of the Knowledge of Good and Bad	Experience both Garden Life and Light and Death and Darkness	To "eat" (enjoy) the Light Experience or the Dark Experience	Live more in the Garden Light or Die more in Darkness

Consciousness and Unconsciousness

To the degree that we are conscious, to that degree, we are continually aware of the dynamics in the above chart. That enables us to choose to evolve in a fulfilled life. To the degree that we are unconscious, to that degree, we wander through life and end up automatically more dead in darkness.

Exercise:

Question for Reflection: When you are very upset, do you know things as sublimely "life" and as "perfect-as-is?"

My answer: I have learned that deep-down I know things as "life;" however, that perception often is not immediately apparent to me. At those times, I can be consumed with bad and good and with death and darkness. Unless I go apart, become still in the moment, and let Spirit inspire me to know all as perfect-as-is and sublime, I will automatically choose to devolve more in death and darkness.

In situations where I have developed deep hate for someone or something, it can take me a long time to know the person or event sublimely as "life," and "perfect-as-is."

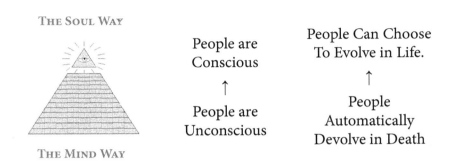

THE SOUL WAY

People are Conscious

↑

People are Unconscious

THE MIND WAY

People Can Choose To Evolve in Life.

↑

People Automatically Devolve in Death

JESUS AND THE TWO TREES

In *The Gospel of Thomas* (Saying 19), Jesus agrees with Eve that we know with two trees. Our challenge is to use them properly so that in every moment we can choose between their fruits (Experiences).

You have two trees in Paradise[1]	[1] *Two trees in paradise:* Two trees in the Garden of Eden.[9]
Which move not in summer or in winter[2]	[2] *Which move not in summer or winter:* Which are available in easy and hard times.
And their leaves are not discovered down.[3]	[3] *Their leaves are not discovered down:* Their ideas are always available.
He who will know them[4]	[4] *He who will know them:* He who will know how to use them correctly.
Will take a taste not of death.[5]	[5] *Will take a taste, not of death:* Will not sample the Dark Experience.

---

9   *Two Trees:* Our current text says "five trees;" however, that probably is a copyist mistake.

According to Jesus, we are born into the Garden Experience eating of the Tree of the Knowledge of Life. However, eventually, we learn to eat of the Tree of the Knowledge of Good and Bad. Then, we can choose to continue to live in the Garden or in the Dark Experience.

KNOWING THE SUBLIME

We can know "life" or the sublime in anyone or anything, even when faced with the most horrible events. For example, when a family member thinks of his parents going to the gas chamber during the Holocaust, he may be overcome with horror, depression, and other emotions arising from knowing that situation only as "bad." To heal according to the Garden Command, the person must also know the sublime or perfect-as-is of those people going to their death and of the guards who are murdering them.

That is not easy to do. However, that is Eve's secret to emotional health—to uncover the sublime in any person or event. To do that, a person must be one with Spirit, which will lead him out of his obsession with primarily knowing all as bad and good. When a person can do that, he can choose to eat the light fruit (Experience) or the dark one.

As an example, let us consider a mother who has just given birth to a deformed baby. When she sees the baby for the first time, she presents herself with two fruits: the Dark Experience (anger, grieving, depression, etc.) and the Garden Experience (oneness with the baby, joy, stillness in the now, etc.). She then chooses which experience to eat (enjoy). One will lead her and her child to fulfillment and life, the other, to them devolving into emotional misery and death.

That mother may not experience the Garden Experience with her baby immediately. She may need to retreat and wait for inspiration to guide her into the Garden. Slowly, Spirit will reveal how to love the child unconditionally. Then, if she persists, she will be led to guard herself and the child against people who see the child differently.

CHILD DEVELOPMENT

After birth, most babies seem to choose most often to eat the life fruit rather than the dead one. Gradually, though, adults teach the child that he is "bad" if he does not possess certain things, believe the true religious faith, possess the proper skin color, looks, behaviors, social standing, etc. Each time the adult tells him that he is "bad," to remain in the Garden, he must choose to reveal himself and others as perfect-as-is.

Those children who submit to adults' false values become divided between their core, real, divine self, and the false selves they have adopted. When they do that, they experience that divide within as anxiety, worry, and fear arising out of pretending to be what they are not. Eve, Jesus, and Buddha call that state living "death." It is the Dark Experience.

Jesus associates inner division with the Dark Experience many times in *The Gospel of Thomas.* An example is in Saying 61:

"When
he
should come to be
destroyed[1]

[1]*When he should come to be destroyed:* When he should destroy his false selves.

He
will be full
of light.[2]

[2]*He will be full of light:* He will be full of divine light.

When
however
he
should come to be
divided[3]

[3]*When, however, he should come to be divided:* When one should come to be divided between his real and false selves, and between his real self and the real selves of others.

He
will be full
of darkness.[4]

[4]*He will be full of darkness:* He will full of living death.

Buddha and the Wise

Buddha (Ch. 7) agrees with Jesus:

The wise man
becomes a light
pure, brilliant, and free.

Most, if not all, children, hate division and death. But then, they learn how to distract themselves from their emotional pain. Later as adults, they will call their agonizing death experience "normal." When that happens, the Garden experience will become more of a vague memory.

Buddha taught that a wise person recognizes that as a child, he was taught by adults to enjoy the fruit of the Tree of the Knowledge of Good and Bad. Those caretakers gave him lessons about how to eat the feelings that come from thinking he is better than others because of his faith, his appearance, his intelligence, his class status, his skin color, his race, his …on and on. The wise person then destroys those illusions about himself to be "light, pure, brilliant, and free" in a dark and dead world.

Eve's Emotional Health Secret

Eve tells us that when we eat the fruit of the Knowledge of Good and Bad, we enjoy the experience of depression, anger, regret, worry, loneliness, and other emotional lows and false highs. If we did not have some sense of pleasure with those experiences, we would not choose them. Thus, *we always choose between two types of enjoyments:* the Garden Experience and the Dark Experience. The Garden may not be right in front of us; however, if we destroy our illusions, it will come forth. Then, we can choose it.

Thus, the secret to emotional health (for which governments are spending billions today) Eve discovered over four thousand years ago. It is the Garden Command. Today, few people know that. Consequently, patients spend a lot of money and time with therapists who do not teach them how to eat of the Tree of the Knowledge of Life.

Exercise:

Question for Reflection: Remember a personal tragedy. Did you know it as bad, good, perfect-as-is, full of life, or full of death?

My answer: My immediate reaction was to know the event and those who caused the tragedy as very bad. I enjoyed eating that darkness.

Exercise:

Questions for Reflection:

1. Identify someone who is, in some way, your enemy. Know that person with the Tree of the Knowledge of Good and Bad. In other words, primarily focus on the good and bad in that person. Then, enjoy the Dark Experience. How do you like your life?

2. Now, know that person with the Tree of the Knowledge of Life. In other words, go apart, become still, and let Spirit guide you to know your enemy as perfect-as-is who does good-bad things. Then, enjoy the Garden Experience. How do you like your life?

My answers:

1. Identify someone who is, in some way, your enemy. Know that person with the Tree of the Knowledge of Good and Bad. In other words, primarily focus on the bad in that person. Then, enjoy the Dark Experience. How do you like your life? **My answer:** On one level, I enjoy feeling superior to the other person. On a deeper level, I am miserable.

2. Now, know that person with the Tree of the Knowledge of Life. In other words, go apart, become still, and let Spirit guide you to know your enemy as perfect-as-is who does good and bad things. Then, enjoy the Garden Experience. How do you like your life? **My answer:** I like my life and myself, in other words, I enjoy eating the Light Experience.

Exercise:

Questions for Reflection:

1. Identify a person you know well who strongly lives death.

2. Identify a person you know well who strongly lives life.

My answers:

1. Identify a person you know well who strongly lives death. **My answer:** Whoever that person is, at some level, you do not feel comfortable around him. He brings you down. He does not model how you want to live.

2. Identify a person you know well who strongly lives life. **My answer:** Whoever that person is, at some level, you feel at home with him. He raises your spirits. He is either a child or an adult who lives from his child-center.

CHAPTER FOUR

THE GARDEN OF EDEN ALLEGORY: OUR WOMAN

INTRODUCTION

Eve has told us that Spirit creates each of us:

- With divine life.

- In the Garden of Eden.

- Knowing that our job is to nurture and guard our Garden.

- With an in-born command to eat of the Tree of the Knowledge of Life and not eat of the Tree of the Knowledge of Good and Bad

Now, Eve will tell us that we are still incomplete. We need something else to be in the Garden every moment of our lives.

OUR IN-FRONT HELPMATE

Being-Gods
said,

"It
is not good

That
the person
should be alone;

Therefore
I
will make a helpmate
in front of that one.

(Gen 2:18)

I will make a helpmate in front of that one:

From a personal point of view, the Allegory is about each of us. Thus, we are compelled to ask, "Because we are born with so much, why do we each need a "helpmate," and further, one who is "in front" of each of us?

The standard answer given by people for thousands of years who have studied this allegory is: Spirit first created a man, and he needs a woman to complement his abilities and to have his children. But that is reading into the text. At this point, we don't know if the person is a man or woman. Further, as an allegory that applies to everyone, Eve tells us that a woman also needs a helpmate.

But no one to my knowledge has explained why that helpmate needs to be "in front" of each person. Why not behind one or at one's side?

Let us seek our answers by studying the text. The author has said that the person has two functions: to "nourish" and to "guard" the Garden Experience (Genesis 2:15). So, I ask you, the reader, "Which of these two tasks does a man do best, and in which does a woman have more expertise?"

When I ask that question of people, most say that a woman is better at nourishing and that a man is better at guarding.

Two more questions: "Does the woman 'nourish' best by knowing with the Tree of the Knowledge of Bad and Good, or the Tree of the Knowledge of Life?" And "does the man 'guard' best by knowing with the Tree of the Knowledge of Bad and Good, or the tree of the Knowledge of Life?"

Most people say that a woman nourishes best by using the Tree of the Knowledge of Life to love all unconditionally. Also, they say that a man is a natural guard because he knows how to combat a "bad" threat with a "good" saving strategy.

Therefore, a perfect team consists of a woman to nourish and a man to guard. When a woman is "in front," she uses the Tree of the Knowledge of Life to love unconditionally All as perfect-as-is. The man, then, has something to guard. If the man is "in front," he will use the Tree of the Knowledge of Good and Bad to guard what exists. As a result, he will not permit the woman to grow in unconditionally love.

OUR FEMININE AND MASCULINE

The author *humorously* tells us that our all-knowing Spirit has caused a problem. This Being has created a male person who only knows with the Tree of the Knowledge of Good and Bad; therefore, the person needs a female "in front" to know with the Tree of the Knowledge of Life. That is the only way that the person can nurture the Garden Experience

So, Eve tells us allegorically that we *each* need a woman to nourish and a man to guard. Fortunately, *we each have two sides or abilities,* one is right-brain feminine, and the other is left-brain masculine. To develop ourselves in the Garden, we first, make nourishing unconditional love with our woman primary, and then, we make guarding with our man secondary. In other words, soul-knowing with our woman before we mind-know with our man.

The Garden Allegory appears to be about two people, but *it is about one person* who represents each of us. Everyone is born with two sides, one feminine and the other masculine—one to nourish our Garden and the other to guard it. We need to develop those two abilities to remain in or return to the Garden.

THE CREATION OF OUR WOMAN

Eve has shown us that Spirit has blundered by creating a person who is all masculine (in allegories, gods can be goofy). He can guard but not nourish. Let us see how Spirit corrects the situation (Genesis 2:21-23):

Being-Gods
caused a trance
to fall upon the person.

And then,
that One
took one
of his ribs

And
closed up its place
with flesh.

Then
Being-Gods
made a woman
from the rib
of the person.

Being-Gods caused a trance to fall upon the person: Again, the person right now is all man. He needs a sensitive, loving woman "in front." However, his man guards what is as "good" and sees any changes to the present situation as "bad." Therefore, for a person to obtain a woman, he needs to put his guarding man into a kind of "trance." Then, Spirit can create his feminine side with her ability to love unconditionally.

Being-Gods took one of his ribs and closed up its place with flesh.

Rib: We can translate the Hebrew word 'tsela' as "rib" or "plank" or "something hard and strong." A rib is the symbol of the male side of the person.

Flesh: Soft femininity

Being-Gods took one of his ribs and closed up its place with flesh. Spirit removed some of the masculine, hard, macho guarding and put in its place some soft-flesh feminine unconditional love.

Then, Being-Gods made a woman from the rib of the person. Spirit made a soft, nurturing feminine side from the strong masculine side.

The historical interpretation: Spirit created the first male person. Then, Spirit created a woman from the man. In that way, Spirit created two people.

The general allegorical meaning: We were all birthed with two sides: a male side that knows All with the Tree of the Knowledge of Good and Bad and a female side that knows All with the Tree of the Knowledge of Life. Our male side guards and our female side nourishes ourselves and everyone else.

The practical, personal allegorical meaning: Sometimes, a person finds himself in the Dark Experience because his male side is "in front" knowing things primarily as good and bad. To put his women in front, he must put his male guarding side in a trance (make him second in command). The person can then empower (create) his woman's side to be in front, knowing All as perfect-as-is life.

For example, if we say to ourselves, "This is a bad day," we will find ourselves in the Dark Experience. To get out of it, we can go to someplace quiet to reflect and to say to our man, "Hush, stop evaluating the day as good and bad. (In that way, we put him in a "trance"). Then, we can open to empower our woman to know the day as perfect-as-is life. When that happens, she will fill us with unconditional love for things our man called "bad." Then, we can choose to eat (enjoy) experiencing All as "bad" or "perfect-as-is." Our man will then guard the Light or Dark Experience (fruits) that we have chosen by pointing out the bad and good ways that we might proceed.

THE TRICK

When I am in the Dark Experience, it often seems impossible to be in the Light Experience in my present situation. So, in that case, I must force myself to go physically to someplace where I can open my heart to experience All as perfect-as-is. Fortunately, I live three blocks from the ocean and 100 meters from my trail up into the mountains.

After I pack a lunch and water and go to one of those retreats, I am usually able to allow Spirit to guide me to putting my male side in a trance so that my female side can love all unconditionally.

When in a deep Dark Experience, I may have to return to the mountains and sea many times because my ego fights for its life. Wow! Putting that guy to sleep and enabling my woman sometimes exhausts me psychologically and physically. But, I always discover that the difficult transition to a higher level of life is worth all the effort.

JESUS TAUGHT THE GARDEN COMMAND

In *The Gospel of Thomas* (Saying 25), we learn that Jesus agrees with Eve concerning using the Garden Command properly to grow in life and light.

Love your brother[1]	[1]*Brother:* Every person
Like your soul;[2]	[2]*Love your brother like your soul:* Have the same unconditional love for every person as you do for your divine self.
Guard him[3]	[3]*Guard him:* Protect him from anyone who does not unconditionally love him. Also, protect him to the degree that he does not unconditionally love himself.
Like the pupil of your eye.[4]	[4]*Like the pupil of your eye:* Like your most precious, intuitive third-eye.

In this poem, we see that Jesus taught Eve's message: Unconditionally love with your woman first, then guard with your masculine side. In this book, I will call that healing attitude towards oneself and others, "wise-love."

TYPES OF LOVE

To understand wise-love, we need to see it in the context of two other kinds of false love, "naïve love," and "guarded love."

Naïve love: It is to love a person or situation unconditionally without guarding him or it. We stop guarding when we do not embrace the responsibility of noticing the strengths and limitations of the person or situation that we face. When we do that, we naively love a person or situation as totally safe, when that is rarely the complete case. As a result, we will eventually be disappointed and perhaps, harmed.

For example, when our inner woman loves an abuser, she will know the divine in him. That can trap her. She may be so entranced by the inner beauty of the other person that she fails to use her male side to guard her against the abuser's destructive thinking and behavior.

We are all naïve lovers at times. We want to think positively about others so that we can enjoy them. In that way, we will not be a negative burden on ourselves and the world. As a result, we may do the easy thing and refuse to empower our man to warn us of the other person's shortcomings—which everyone possesses.

Guarded love: It is to love another person or situation on the condition that the individual or event benefits us. We do not unconditionally love the other person or event. Instead, we pretend unconditional love to get what we want. That is living a lie that puts us in the Dark Experience.

A guarded person puts his man "in front" to be on the watch continually for the bad and good in another and the situation. When he does that, he will not experience unconditional love. Instead, he will live a lonely, angry life seeking unconditional love nourishment.

A person with his inner man out front cannot be sensitive to the divine life in people. For example, as a parent, a guarded man may reluctantly hug his children. He may also suppress his emotions so much that he is like a robot. In a romantic relationship, he will not please his partner nor himself. Deep down, he will be alone, aloof, and sealed off from himself and the other person.

A person who leads with his masculine degrades, disciplines, persecutes, and even kills without feminine compassion. Because he often appears to be strong, many people feel safe around such a mean person. In difficult or confusing times, people dead in the "world" choose such a leader.

Summary

Types of Love

Naïve Love	One loves himself and others without clearly discerning his own, or another's limitations and strengths. When he does that, he sets himself up for being disappointed and for being manipulated. He will be a weak, foolish parent, partner, or leader.
Guarded Love	One is careful to love because he is aware that another can hurt him. The guarded person demands things before loving. Doing that will prevent him from being intimate. He can be a cruel leader without compassion.
Wise-Love	One first, affirms the unique but common-to-all soul-life in himself and another, and second, guards against the limitations and strengths of others.

The Soul Way

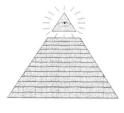

The Mind Way

A person wisely-loves All
↑
A person <u>naively loves</u> and does not guard

A person wisely-loves All
↑
A person <u>guards</u> and does not unconditionally love

EXERCISE:

QUESTIONS FOR REFLECTION: Which are you most?

1. A generous person who lets people abuse you (a naïve lover)?

2. A guarded person who holds others at a distance (a guarded lover)?

3. A person who is both generous to people and who holds them accountable (a wise lover)?

My answer: We are all at times naïve lovers, guarded lovers, and wise-lovers.

EXERCISE:

QUESTIONS FOR REFLECTION: Think of a time when you approached a person with your guard up, that is, with strong, male skepticism about his intentions.

1. Were you able to offer a genuinely warm smile?

2. Were you open to listening to them?

3. Do you think that you evaluated them accurately?

MY ANSWERS:

Think of a time when you approached a group or person with strong male skepticism about their intentions.

1. Were you able to offer a genuinely warm smile? **My answer:** No. I may have smiled, but I was not genuinely friendly.

2. Were you open to listening to them? **My answer:** It was difficult because I had already made up my mind about them.

3. Do you think that you evaluated them accurately? **My answer:** No. Bias in, bias out.

EXERCISE:

QUESTIONS FOR REFLECTION:

1. Does an extreme conservative lead with his masculine or feminine?

2. Does an extreme liberal lead with his masculine or feminine?

3. Does a balanced leader (e.g., politician, parent, etc.) lead with his masculine or feminine?

MY ANSWERS:

1. Does an extreme conservative lead with his masculine or feminine? **My answer:** He leads with his masculine. He may never implement policies out of compassion for people unlike him.

2. Does an extreme liberal lead with his masculine or feminine? **My answer:** He leads with his feminine and may not follow with his masculine to hold people accountable.

3. Does a balanced leader (e.g., politician, parent, etc.) lead with his masculine or feminine? **My answer:** He leads with his feminine and follows with his masculine.

EXERCISE:

QUESTIONS FOR REFLECTION: Which of the following options best describe your definition of what it means to "forgive" another?

1. To love the other person unconditionally.

2. To make excuses for the other person's words and actions?

3. To overlook what the other person said and did?

4. To forget that the event ever happened?

5. To hold the other person accountable?

6. To unconditionally love the other person and hold him accountable?

My answer: Number six.

EXERCISE

QUESTIONS FOR REFLECTION: When we look at social institutions today, such as religions and political parties:

1. Are most leaders, men or women? Why?

2. Do we see more masculine division and conflict or more feminine oneness and cooperation in society? Why?

3. Do leaders generally lead with unconditional love and follow with ways to protect everyone, or do they lead with words and actions that divide and rarely follow with ways to unconditionally love?

MY ANSWERS:

When we look at social institutions today, such as religions and political parties:

1. Are most leaders, men or women? Why? **My answer:** Most leaders are men, because, in general, society devalues our feminine side.

2. Do we see more masculine division and conflict or more feminine oneness and cooperation in society? **My answer:** We see not only more masculine conflicts, but people using their masculine to enjoy the discrimination, persecution, and the killing of others.

3. Do leaders generally lead with unconditional love and follow with ways to protect everyone, or do they lead with words and actions that divide and rarely follow with ways to unconditionally love? **My answer:** They most often lead with words that divide and attack. For example, many leaders say such things as "These immigrants will destroy what we have built." We seldom hear leaders lead with their woman and follow with their man by saying things like: "We need to love immigrants as our brothers or sisters, and at the same time, find a way to protect what we have built."

EXERCISE

QUESTIONS FOR REFLECTION: Think of a person who has hurt you deeply. Or think of a loss or failure that has caused you great pain. Notice how the person or situation haunts you. You may be in Post-Traumatic Stress.

1. Why are you in emotional pain?

2. How do you get out of emotional pain?

MY ANSWERS:

1. Why are you in emotional pain? **My answer:** Our macho, guarding man is out front judging the person or situation as "bad."

2. How do you get out of emotional pain? **My answer:** We will suffer the rest of your life when bad haunts us unless we put our man in a trance, put our unconditionally loving woman in front, and choose to eat the Garden Experience.

That is easier to say than to do it. We all suffer from PTSD to some extent. To conquer it, I do the following:

Step One: When rested, I go alone to a beautiful and peaceful place. There, I resolve to stop running from the pain and to go through it. I also resolve to do the impossible, to love it All unconditionally.

Step Two: I bring the person and situation to mind and re-experience it all, especially the pain. If the pain is too much, I imagine the situation or person very distant from me.

Step Three: I open to be guided by Spirit to love it All unconditionally, the person, the situation, and all the suffering that happened. I do not permit any thought to come to mind if it is not flowing through my soul in love. I avoid thinking from my mind, which judges all as good or bad. I patiently suffer and wait and watch and plead. I open to see myself as letting go of my guarding ego-man. I long for my woman to come and guide me.

Step Four: I sometimes find it helpful to say to the person or event in my imagination: "You are there, and I am here. I love it all." When I become present with myself and separated from what caused me the suffering, I know that I have released myself from the control of who or what I hated.

Step Six: I evaluate. I use my man to see the good and bad in the situation or person that caused me the trauma.

Step Seven: I enjoy the Garden Experience.

Later, I repeat the exercise by bringing the situation or person closer to me in my imagination. Eventually, I can stand and face it or him up close. Then, I will feel present with myself in wise-love. I always experience that the PTSD slowly disappears, and I am living more in the Light Experience.

I find that this process takes patience. Further, I feel at times as if I am turning myself inside out to love what I hate. When I have spent days and years rehashing "bad," it takes time to get free and experience it all as perfect-as-is. When I feel the release, I enjoy it and reward myself in some way.

Psychological Healing

Eve has just explained how we heal deep psychological wounds: We put our man in a trance and find a way to put our woman out front unconditionally loving what we dislike or hate. Then, relaxed and detached from our obsession with "bad," we can choose to be in the Light or Dark Experience. Finally, we can use our man to accurately assess the good and bad in a person or event that caused us so much upset.

CHAPTER FIVE

THE GARDEN OF EDEN ALLEGORY: HOW WE OBTAIN FREE CHOICE

INTRODUCTION

Eve has told us that Spirit birthed a person with only a masculine side; therefore, he cannot eat of the Tree of the Knowledge of Life. Spirit recognized the problem and gave the man his feminine way of knowing. Now the person can use both his woman to nurture him in the Garden and his man to guard him against temptations to leave that fulfilled life. Let us read more of the allegory to find out whether the person chooses to stay in the Garden or to leave it.

THE PERSON'S SNAKE

Now, Eve introduces us to our snake (Gen 3:1):

The snake
was more crafty
than
any living thing
of the field

Which
Being-Gods
had made.

The snake
said to the woman,
"Indeed,
Gods
said,

'You
can eat of the trees
of the garden.'"

Snake: In many allegories, animals represent our abilities and traits. An ox, for example, is our stubborn, often dumb persistence. Our snake inspires us in "crafty" ways. In other words, he will trick us into doing something.

The snake said to the woman, "Indeed, Gods said, 'You can eat of the trees of the garden.'"

The snake does not lie. We *can* eat from either Tree. However, if we choose to disobey the Garden Command and eat of the Tree of the Knowledge of Good and Bad, we will psychologically die on the Mind Way.

Now, we see that the snake set a trap. He wants the woman to understand that eating of the Tree of the Knowledge of Good and Bad is perfect-as-is. She can see anything that way. So, he deceives her craftily, not by lying, but by stating the truth: the person does have the ability to eat of both trees.

Let us see how our woman responds to the snake (Gen 3:2-3):

The woman
said to the snake,

"Of the fruit
of the Tree
(in the middle)[1]
of the Garden[2]
we
may eat;

[1]*In the middle:* This phrase is implied. Eve tells us that the Tree of the Knowledge of Life is "in the middle" in Gen 2:9.

[2]*Of the fruit of the Tree in the middle of the Garden:* That is the Tree of the Knowledge of Life, which is in the center of our being.

> But
> of the fruit
> of the Tree
> that
> is
> not in the middle
> of the Garden,[3]
>
> The Gods
> said,
> 'You
> shall not eat
> from it
> Or
> you
> will die.'"[4]

[3] *The tree which is not in the middle:* The Tree of the Knowledge of Bad and Good.

[4] *You will die:* You will live in psychological and spiritual pain on the Mind Way.

A great response from our woman. She isn't going to permit the snake to fool her. She understands that the person *can* eat of both trees, but one will lead to a living death.

The situation: Spirit birthed the person into "life" in the Garden of Eden. He did not give the person an experience of "death" on the Mind Way. Therefore, the person cannot choose between life and death.

Spirit gave the person a command to blindly eat of the Tree of the knowledge of Life and to not eat of the Tree of the Knowledge of Good and Bad. Unless the person experiences both life and death, he has no *free choice,* which is necessary for him to evolve fully into the divine life that Spirit has given him.

For example, a baby is born in the Light Experience. He is innocent because he has not chosen to eat the Dark Experience. At some point, perhaps imitating his parents, he will taste death. He might do that by lying for the first time and experiencing darkness. Then, he will know both life and death enjoyments. That will enable him to possess free choice. From then on, he will develop his character by choosing in every moment to evolve or devolve, to become more alive or dead, to eat of this Tree or that one.

Let us see how our crafty snake responds (Gen 3:-5):

The snake
said to the woman,

"You
will not die

And
die!

For
the Gods
know

That
on the day
you
eat from it,

Your eyes
will be opened,

And
you
will be Gods
knowing good and bad."

The snake said to the woman, "You will not die and die! For the Gods know that on the day you eat from it, your eyes will be opened."

"You will not die and die! You cannot die on the Mind Way unless you choose to live that way. Right now, you do not possess free choice.

Your eye will be opened. You will have free choice when you open your third-eye.

The snake said to the woman: You will be (one of the) Gods, knowing good and bad.

The situation: The person is undeveloped divine life in the Garden. When his eyes are opened, he will possess the ability to choose between the Light and Dark Experiences. Then, he will be fully one of the "Gods."

Let us see what the woman does (Gen 3:6-7):

When the woman saw the Tree	[1] *When the woman saw the Tree and that it was good for food:* When our female side intuitively knew the Tree of the Knowledge of Good and Bad as perfect-as-is and that it provides an enjoyable Dark Experience,
And that it was good for food,[1]	
compelling to the eyes,[2]	[2] *When the woman saw that the Tree was compelling to the eyes:* When the woman realized that the Tree of the Knowledge of Good and Bad was enticing…
and a tree to be desired for wisdom,[3]	[3] *When the woman saw that the Tree is to be desired for wisdom:* When the woman saw that the Tree of the Knowledge of Good and Bad was essential for obtaining the information to guard the person,
She took its fruit and ate it;[4]	[4] *She took its fruit and ate it:* She chose the Dark Experience and enjoyed the death-drama of living in the past and future on a roller coaster of emotions.
And she gave it also to her man,[5]	[5] *And he gave it to her man:* And she presented the Dark Experience to the man as important for him to know.
And he ate it.[6]	[6] *And he ate it:* And the person's masculine side enjoyed the Dark Experience also.

The woman saw the Tree was good for food, compelling to the eyes, and a Tree to be desired for wisdom: The person's woman realized that the Tree of the Knowledge of Good and Bad provided many pleasurable insights.

We always choose between two pleasures. The Tree of the Knowledge of Life provides one kind — the Tree of the Knowledge of Good and Bad yields another. So, the women saw that the pleasures of the Mind Way, although ultimately destructive to self & others, were perfect-as-is.

She took the fruit and ate it: She ate and enjoyed the Dark Experience.

"And she gave it to her man, and he ate it." The person's feminine soul-side presented the masculine mind-side with an enjoyable experience; so he ate it. Now, both of them knew that there are two ways to live.

Exercise

Question for Reflection: Did the person with his/her man and woman sin when they ate the forbidden fruit?

My answer: No. Before eating the fruit, the person did not know the difference between a Light and Dark Experience; so, he had no free choice. You need that to sin.

When the person through his man and woman ate the fruit of the Tree of the Knowledge of Good and Bad for the first time, he learned the implications of living in the Dark Experience. Now, he can choose each minute between living in one or the other Experience.

Exercise

QUESTIONS FOR REFLECTION: Please answer the following questions that are designed to help us understand the pleasure of eating the Dark Experience.

1. Have you ever enjoyed talking about another person in a way that made you seem "good" and him "bad?"

2. Have you ever done anything unloving?

3. Have you ever not exercised when you knew it would be healthy for you?

4. Do people enjoy playing video games in which they kill the bad guys?

5. Why do children enjoy teasing other children into tears?

6. Have you ever engaged in sex out of lust?

7. Have you ever lied?

My answer: In all of the situations that those questions describe, I do something "bad" because my snake tricks me into thinking that they are an enjoyable and a good way to live. I do enjoy doing those things, but deep down, I know that I have entered the Dark Experience. Then, I may do something else "bad" to feel better. And so, as I repeat that process, I become numb to feeling "bad" and begin automatically to seek the Dark Experience rather than the Light Experience.

Summary

The person's man and woman did not sin by eating the forbidden "fruit." Instead, they obtain the dignity of possessing divine, free choice.

As an allegory, Eve tells us that we sometimes need to experience darkness to know its pleasures. For example, a person may go into a decadent night club for the first time and enjoy the down in false highs. After that, he can choose to sin by seeking false high environments or to grow in life by finding situations where people are on the Soul Way.

Both the Garden and the Dark Experience provide pleasure. Our snake manipulates us to choose the latter by ensuring that we cannot see through cleverly designed, camouflaged, ultimately empty enjoyments.

CHAPTER SIX

THE GARDEN OF EDEN ALLEGORY: HOW WE SIN

INTRODUCTION

The next part (Gen 3:7) explains the result of eating of the fruit of the Tree of the Knowledge of Good and Bad for the first time:

After
they
ate the fruit,

The eyes
of both
of them
were opened,[1]

And
they
knew their nakedness.[2]

[1] *Then the eyes of both of them were opened:* Then the person had free choice because he could distinguish between the two opposed enjoyable experiences.

[2] *And they knew their nakedness:* And they knew that they were divinely perfect-as-is **without** sin, just like a new-born child. To be "naked" is to be oneself.

Then, the eyes of both of them were opened. Then, they had developed free choice.

And they knew their nakedness. And they knew that they were essentially perfect-as-is life and *not* bad.

JESUS AND NAKEDNESS

The word "naked" means to be oneself, divine life, and nothing else. To put on garments means to identify with people and things rather than one's core life. When we do that, we become false. Jesus explains the meaning of the "naked" metaphor in *The Gospel of Thomas* (Saying 37):

"When
you
should strip yourselves
naked[1]
without being ashamed[2]

And
you
take your garments[3]

And
you
put them
on the earth[4]

under your feet[5]

Like
those little
small children[6]

And
you
trample them;[7]

Then
you
will peer upon the son
of He
who
lives[8]

[1] *When you should strip yourselves naked:* When you remove your false identities; when you stop thinking that your appearance, money, theology, politics, skin color, race, nationality, traditions, intelligence, etc. makes you special, good, and saved.

[2] *Without being ashamed:* Without worrying about whether you conform to the expectations of others.

[3] *Garments:* False identities.

[4] *And you put them on the earth:* To put garments on the earth is to bring into consciousness one's false identifications and the harm they cause to oneself and others.

[5] *Feet:* What we stand on for conviction. Our principles.

[6] *Little, small children:* Children and adults who are themselves, that is, who have no false identities.

[7] *Trample them:* See those clothes (false identities) as foolish and useless. To trample is to demean what gave one false life.

[8] *You will peer upon the son of He Who lives:* You will third-eye reveal to yourself that you are the son or daughter of God.

And
you
will come to be
afraid
not.[9]

[9] *You will come to be afraid not:* You will not be afraid of people rejecting you. For example, if you do not identify with your appearance, and people call you "ugly," you will not feel rejected. Instead, you will be able to choose to wise-love them (love them unconditionally and guard yourself and others against their prejudices).

When born, we are naked, beautiful innocence without pretentions. Then, we learn *not* to be ourselves by identifying with people, beliefs, and things that meet the expectations of others.

JESUS MENTAL HEALTH SECRET

In the previous poem, Jesus states that the way to live without fear, worry, anxiety, depression, etc. is to remove our false selves. We create them when we identify with anything other than our core, *naked* life.

For example, if a person identifies with his reputation or religious faith (garments), the opinions of others about him or his beliefs become personal. Then, deep down, he may feel afraid, rejected, unsafe, or unsaved. To avoid those feelings, he may defend and promote his reputation or beliefs as he does himself.

However, if he would 1) take-off (de-identify) with his reputation or faith, 2) be willing to be naked (be himself) in front of people, 3) suffer the consequences, and 4) wise-love himself and all involved, he would be free of the anxiety of defending and promoting himself. Finally, he would guard himself by trusting others only to the degree that they walk around being their naked selves.

Jesus explains how we must suffer rejection to become naked in the following poem from *The Gospel of Thomas* (Saying 21):

Mary
said to Jesus:

"Your disciples

They
resemble
whom?"

Jesus
responded:

"They
resemble
small children[1]

dwelling in a field[2]

[1]*Small children:* Those who are naked of false identities.

[2]*Dwelling in a field:* A "field" is one's environment. It could be a family, work situation, or peer group. One "dwells" in that field by putting on the clothes (false identities) that everyone expects.

[3]*Children dwelling in a field which is not theirs:* Naked ones who conform superficially to the expectations of others. For example, they may celebrate a family tradition without identifying with it.

Which
is
not theirs.[3]

When
they
should come
Namely
the
lords of the field[4]

[4]*Lords of the field:* Those on the Mind Way who want to control the thinking and actions of others in this situation.

They
will say this:
'Release our field
back to us.'[5]

[5]*Release our field back to us:* Stop being independent. Instead, prove that you identify with our beliefs, values, and customs.

And
they
will strip naked
in their presence[6]

[6]*They will strip naked in their presence:* The child-adults will become their real selves in the presence of everyone.

So that
it
be given back
to them.[7]

[7]*So that it be given back to them:* So that those clothed on the Mind Way can live falsely and suffer the consequences—which may lead them eventually to want the Garden rather than the Dark Experience.

In this poem, Jesus explains that to be ourselves, we often must resist the pressure to conform. For example, in a "field" (situation) where everyone identifies with their political beliefs, a person on the Soul Way, who identifies only with what seems true to him, will most likely be seen as a non-conformist. That could cause the leaders of the "field" to, in some way, demand conformity. When that happens, the person on the Soul Way may suffer rejection or worse, such as discrimination in employment and social standing, or even physical persecution and death.

All of us are challenged to be our naked selves against the expectations of others. Even when alone, we measure our worth against how others have perceived us in the past or how they might in the future. So, to choose to be naked takes courage. However, if one does that, he lives as himself, free and unafraid.

BUDDHA AND NAKEDNESS

Buddha calls the act of putting on garments becoming "attached" to people and things. By extension, to become naked is to be detached. We read that in the Dhammapada (Ch. 15):

> *Be free from attachment*
> *and*
> *experience the sublime joy*
> *of the Way*
> *(of the Soul)*

A keyword in Buddha's poem is "attachment." When we identify with anyone or anything for our meaning, purpose and worth— other than our unique presentation of our divine self in the world— we become "attached" to what we are not. That leads us to die by promoting and defending with regret and worry what is unimportant.

HOW WE SIN AND BECOME EMOTIONALLY SICK

Let us read whether the person with his woman and man decided to remain real and in the Garden or to be false, which would force them out of it into emotional sickness.

Then, by sewing fig leaves together:

Leaves: A "leaf" is a belief on a tree of knowledge. In this case, it is the Tree of the Knowledge of Good and Bad.

Then by sewing fig leaves together…: Then, the woman and man by adopting a system of beliefs about how they are "good" as opposed to others who are "bad…

They made for themselves aprons. Then they made for themselves "aprons" (garments or false identities). For example, one can put on fig leaves when he thinks he is important or saved because of his religious, economic, political, family, tribe, or national beliefs.

The sin: The person did not sin the first time he ate the fruit of the Tree of the Knowledge of Good and Bad. Instead, he evolved with free choice. Then, he sinned when he ate the fruit the second time in the process of putting on an apron.

When we are not ourselves, we experience things like insecurity, anxiety, anger, depression, and worthlessness, alternating with false highs. Those are the fruits of the Tree of the Knowledge of Good and Bad that we enjoy. Until we take off all of our aprons, we are doomed to the pleasures of a roller coaster emotional life that comes from promoting and defending what is not essential. When we do decide to de-identify from our garments, then we enjoy the fruit of the Tree of the Knowledge of Life, which is the "sublime joy" that Buddha mentions.

Exercise

Questions for Reflection: To recognize when we put on garments (false selves), think of a time when you were ***not*** yourself in a social setting (a "field").

1. How did being a false affect your feelings?

2. How did being a false affect your thinking?

3. How did being false affect the way you talked to people?

4. Were you living in the past, present, or future?

5. Did you enjoy being false?

6. If you were not enjoying being false, what did you do to relieve your pain?

7. With what did you identify that you were promoting and defending? In other words, what garments (false identities) did you put on? (For example, were you defending and promoting your reputation, your job, your intelligence, your appearance, or …?

8. In the social setting, were you using a single eye to see as Spirit soul-guided you, or two mental eyes to watch yourself and the reactions of others?

9. When you left the social situation, did you feel rested or drained?

10. In that social setting, were you enjoying the Garden or Dark Experience?

11. In that social setting, what was your snake telling you?

MY ANSWERS:

Think of a time when you were **not** yourself in a social setting, that is, in a "field."

1. How did being false affect your feelings? **My answer:** I often feel dirty, inadequate, worried, and anxious.

2. How did being false affect your thinking? **My answer:** I do not think clearly. I am distracted by the task of manipulating myself to control the views of others.

3. How did being false affect the way you talked to people? **My answer:** I laugh inappropriately sometimes and do not say what is really on my mind. My words do not flow.

4. Were you living in the past, present, or future? **My answer:** I refer mentally to the past to not repeat mistakes. I also plan mentally how to ensure future things happen or do not happen.

5. Did you enjoy being false? **My answer:** Yes, and no. I enjoy the false sense of friendship, but deep down, I am miserable.

6. If you were not enjoying being false, what did you do to relieve your pain? **My answer:** I ate myself numb.

7. With what did you identify that you were promoting and defending? In other words, what garments (false identities) did you put on? (For example, were you defending and promoting your reputation, your job, your intelligence, your appearance or what)? **My answer:** My reputation and my most recent project.

8. In the social setting, were you using a single eye to see as Spirit soul-guided you, or two mental eyes to watch yourself and the reactions of others? **My answer:** I was out of touch with soul-guidance. I was totally in my mind using my two eyes.

9. When you left the social situation, did you feel rested or drained? **My answer:** Usually, I was exhausted.

10. In that social setting, were you enjoying the Garden or Dark Experience? **My answer:** The Dark Experience.

11. In that social setting, what was your snake telling you? **My answer:** My snake guided me to see good in being a phony.

EXERCISE

QUESTIONS FOR REFLECTION: Think of a time when you *were your real self* in a social setting.

1. How did being your real self affect your feelings?

2. How did being your real self affect your thinking?

3. How did being your real self affect the way you talked to people?

4. Were you living in the past, present, or future?

5. Did you enjoy being your real self?

6. With what did you identify that you were promoting and defending?

7. In the social setting, were you using a single eye to see as Spirit soul-guided you, or two mental eyes to watch yourself and the reactions of others?

8. When you left the social situation, did you feel rested or drained?

9. In that social setting, were you enjoying the Garden or Dark Experience?

10. In that social setting, what was your snake telling you?

My answers:

1. How did being your real self affect your feelings? **My answer:** I felt refreshingly clean.

2. How did being your real self affect your thinking? **My answer:** My thoughts came naturally.

3. How did being your real self affect the way you talked to people? **My answer:** I was able to express myself well. My words flowed through me.

4. Were you living in the past, present, or future? **My answer:** In the present. I felt powerfully grounded.

5. Did you enjoy being your real self? **My answer:** Very much, even though I was aware that some people did not enjoy me.

6. With what did you identify that you were promoting and defending? **My answer:** My real self. I did not wear a garment.

7. In the social setting, were you using a single eye to see as Spirit soul-guided you, or two mental eyes to watch yourself and the

reactions of others? **My answer:** I was conscious of Spirit guiding me through my single ear and eye, that is, through my intuition.

8. When you left the social situation, did you feel rested or drained? **My answer:** I felt full of energy and love for myself.

9. In that social setting, were you enjoying the Garden or Dark Experience? **My answer:** The Garden Experience.

10. In that social setting, what was your snake telling you? **My answer:** My snake showed me ways I could enjoy being false. I listened to my snake and said, "No, thanks."

EXERCISE

QUESTIONS FOR REFLECTION: Let us examine how we identify with things and people. What do you regard as "sacred?"

1. Your flag?

2. Your religious faith?

3. Your religious building?

4. Your religion's implements?

5. Your religious rituals?

6. Your politics?

7. Your traditions?

8. Your being naked in wise-love of all?

My answer: When I regard anyone or anything as sacred other than being naked in wise-love of All, I become false and die in the Dark Experience.

People regard something as sacred when an individual or group identifies with it. However, Eve and Jesus consider nothing to be sacred except a person who is naked in wise-love of All? He is the holy, cleansed temple in the moment wherever he is. He does not need to go anywhere to adore or be one with Spirit. He is the divine presence in the world.

EXERCISE

QUESTIONS FOR REFLECTION:

1. Today, would Eve be a Jew?

2. Today, would Buddha be a Buddhist?

3. Today, would Jesus be a Christian?

4. Today, would Eve, Buddha, or Jesus, be a liberal? A conservative?

5. Today, would Eve, Buddha, or Jesus, be an Atheist?

My answer: As I read the words of Eve, Buddha, and Jesus, I believe that they would not identify with any organization whose leaders and members taught people to be saved, good, or special for their faith in anything other than being their naked selves. These masters were leading people out of false identifications, not into them. So, to be clear, they would not BE a Jew, Buddhist, Christian, a liberal, a conservative, or an Atheist. They may go to a church, temple, or political meeting, but not **BE** the dogmas taught there.

EXERCISE:

QUESTIONS FOR REFLECTION: Which of the following statements are true for you?

1. I am my spouse.

2. I am my children.

3. I am my friends.

4. I am my country.

5. I am my religious faith.

6. I am my political party.

7. I am my things.

8. I am my appearance.

9. I am my reputation.

10. I am what others think of me.

11. I am my job.

12. I am my gender.

13. I am my race.

14. I am me.

15. I am everyone.

16. I am everyone and everything.

17. I am divine.

MY ANSWER

According to my reading of the words of Eve, Buddha, and Jesus, I cannot *be* numbers 1-13 above *to be* 14-17. The Soul Way is the Way to become nothing but "me." In that Way, "I" become everyone and everything.

Jesus and False Identifications

Jesus composed a wonderful poem in *The Gospel of Thomas* (Saying 114) about how one should not identify even with his gender if he wants to live a full life.

Simon Peter said to them this:

"Make Mary leave us

For women are worthy not of life."[1]

[1]*For women are worthy not of life:* For women are not worthy of being in the Garden of Eden eating of the Tree of the Knowledge of life.

Jesus said this:

"Behold![2]

[2]*Behold:* See intuitively with your third-eye. Do not use your reasoning two eyes primarily.

I myself will lead her[3]

[3]*I, myself, will lead her:* I will empower her by modeling the Soul Way.

So that I might make her male[4]

[4]*So that I might make her male:* So that I might show her how to identify with her core life that is identical to the core life in men. She needs to learn how not to identify primarily with her gender.

So that she might come to be a spirit,[5]

[5]*She might come to be a spirit:* She might come to be one with the divine spirit in herself and all others, regardless of their gender.

She living and resembling you males.[6]

[6]*She resembling you males:* She will be a twin in spirit to any man.

For any woman who makes herself male Will go into the Kingdom of the heavens.[7,8]	[7]*Heavens:* A "heaven" is a high level of knowing, not a place we go to after we physically die. [8]*For any woman who makes herself male will go into the kingdom of the heavens:* For when a woman identifies with the same core, soul life in a man that is also in her, she enters the Garden.

In this poem, Jesus teaches us the only way to grow in the Garden experience: we must evolve to identify with divine life in ourselves and every person. If we identify with something superficial to a person, such as his gender, we identify with a false self in ourselves and him.

Exercise

Questions for Reflection:

1. To be in the Garden, does a man need to become the soul twin of all women?

2. When women are second class citizens in a family, in a company, a nation, or the world, will we solve our problems?

3. When a woman feels soul-essence superior or inferior to one man, will she be fulfilled?

4. When a man feels soul-essence superior or inferior to anyone, will he be fulfilled?

My answers:

1. "To be in the Garden, does a man need to become the soul twin of all women?" **My answer:** Implied in Jesus' poem above, I, as a man, need to identify with the core life in a woman to be fully alive and wise. To the degree that I am the soul-twin of everyone, to that degree, I will be fulfilled in the Garden.

2. When women are second class citizens in a family, in a company, a nation, or the world, will we solve our problems? **My answer:** No. I cannot imagine how we can implement unifying answers to our problems when we are divided from our soul essence and the soul essence of another person.

3. When a woman feels soul-essence superior or inferior to one man, will she be fulfilled? **My answer:** I say, "No." Only to the degree that we are the soul-twins of everyone will we be fulfilled in the Garden and will we save the world.

4. When a man feels soul-essence superior or inferior to anyone, will he be fulfilled? **My answer:** No. I, as a man, will be in dark misery.

EXERCISE

QUESTIONS FOR REFLECTION: Do leaders and members of organizations that teach that people are *essentially* 'good' when they believe or do this, and 'bad' when they believe or do that:

1. Eat of the Tree of the Knowledge of Good and Bad or of the Tree of the Knowledge of Life?

2. Model or refute discriminatory thinking and behavior?

3. Preach hate in the name of love, or love in the name of hate?

4. Foster peace or endless genocides and holocausts?

5. Bring unity or division to the world?

MY ANSWERS:

Do leaders and members of organizations that teach that people are *essentially* 'good' when they believe or do this, and 'bad; when they believe or do that:

1. Eat of the Tree of the Knowledge of Good and Bad or of the Tree of the Knowledge of Life? **My answer:** The Tree of the Knowledge of Good and Bad.

2. Model or refute discriminatory thinking and behavior? **My answer:** As a leader, I would be modeling the darkness that my organization preaches against.

3. Preach hate in the name of love, or love in the name of hate? **My answer:** I would be the hate against which I preach.

4. Foster peace or endless genocides and holocausts? **My answer:** I see these organizations and people and my support of them as the root cause of most suffering in the world.

5. Bring unity or division to the world? **My answer:** As a leader, I would be bringing division to the world.

Jesus and the Source of Division and Its Remedy

Eve has shown us that as soon as we put on clothes (false identities), we divide from being ourselves. We also divide from being one with the divine life in all others. So, our developmental goal is to be one with ourselves and others. Jesus says the same in the following poem from *The Gospel of Thomas* (Saying 61):

> *Salome*
> said to Jesus:
>
> "You
> are
> who
>
> You
> man?
>
> From where
> do
> you
> climb onto my
> dining-bed
>
> And
> you
> eat off of my table?"[1]

[1]*From where...do you eat off of my table:* From what Tree do you choose to dine, from the Tree of the Knowledge of Life or the Tree of the Knowledge of Good and Bad?

Jesus
said to her:

I
am
he

Who
exists out
of He

Who
is
undivided.[2]

[2]*Who exists out of He who is undivided:* Who exists out of Spirit who is one with that Being's real self and with the core life in All.

I
am given outward
of that
of my Father.[3]

[3]*Of that of my Father:* Of that life and wisdom of my Father. I, at my core, am divine.

Salome
responded:

"I
am
your disciple."[4]

[4]*I am your disciple:* I will follow your Soul Way. I will not divide from myself or others by wearing garments (by identifying with a belief system). I also will be my divine self.

Jesus
said:

Because
of your response

I
speak to you
this:

"When
he[5]

[5]*He:* A person seeking more life

should come to be
destroyed[6]

[6]*When he should come to be destroyed:*
When he should destroy his ego
(his collection of false selves) by not
identifying with their underlying beliefs.

He
will be
full
of light.[7]

[7]*Light:* The divine light that
illuminates the darkness in all.

When
however
he
should come to be
divided[8]

[8]*When he should come to be divided:*
When he should come to be divided
between his real and false selves and
between himself and others.

He
will be
full
of darkness.[9]

[9]*Darkness:* The Dark Experience.

JESUS AND THE CAUSE OF SIN

Eve, Buddha, and Jesus have stated that we know that oneness with
ourselves and others leads to emotional health and the peaceful
solving of a problem. So what causes us to be divided? That is the
core question.

To put it another way, why did humanity create religions, political
parties, and other organizations that destructively divide people into
good and bad stereotypes? Jesus' provides his answer in *The Gospel
of Thomas* (Saying 43).

Jesus
responded to his disciples:

You
have come to be
like
those Judeans[1,2]

[1]*Judeans:* They symbolize people
in a religion or other organization
(such as a political party) who divide
people into good ones and bad ones
depending upon whether they adopt
the official doctrine.

[2]*You have come to be like those
Judeans:* You have come to be hateful
dividers on the Mind Way.

For they love the tree[3]	[3]*For they love the tree:* For they love the tree of the Knowledge of Good and Bad. For they love being superior over others that they regard as "bad." In that way, they build up their false sense of personal power.
And they hate its fruit[4]	[4]*And they hate its fruit:* And they hate the resulting Dark Experience.
And they love the fruit[5]	[5]*And they love the fruit:* And they love the oneness of being in the Garden Experience.
And they hate the tree.[6]	[6]*And they hate the tree:* And they hate the Tree of the Knowledge of Life. And they hate being humble and one with others.

This poem describes what I see in societies today: religions, political parties, families, tribes, and social groups whose members adopt a common, good, righteous, better-than-thou belief system. Many in these groups (including me at times), "love" both to see themselves as "good" and to denigrate others who are "bad." Yet, many, like me, hate the resulting suffering in the world.

Summary

The person did *not* sin the first time he ate the fruit of the Tree of the Knowledge of Good and Bad (such as an apple as often portrayed in traditional paintings). Instead, he became fully alive with the ability to choose. After that, the person sinned whenever he put on garments (false identities).

To be clear, Eve, the author says that fundamentally, we can sin in only one way—by choosing to enjoy death. The opposite is also true. We can only evolve in character in one way—by choosing to enjoy life.

THE SOUL WAY

THE MIND WAY

Naked and one with himself and others.
↑
Clothed and divided from himself and others.

The world will be at peace when everyone is naked of their faith in anything but themselves.
↑
The world will be at peace when everyone believes the dogma that my tribes and I believe.

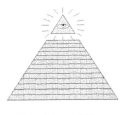

THE SOUL WAY

THE MIND WAY

One with his real divine self.
↑
One with many false selves.

Views everyone as perfect-as-is with strengths & faults.
↑
Views everyone as good or bad.

THE SOUL WAY

THE MIND WAY

Wise-lover of All.
↑
Narcissist
Sociopath
Psychopath.

His decisions will benefit all.
↑
His decisions will benefit himself and those who support him.

CHAPTER SEVEN

THE GARDEN OF EDEN ALLEGORY: WE TESTIFY IN THE GARDEN COURT

INTRODUCTION

The person (who represents each of us) has clothed himself with false identities (garments made up of beliefs about what makes a person safe, saved, and worthy), and as a result, he has chosen to eat the Dark Experience and die. We have all done that. Now, in Genesis 3:8, we will see what happened immediately to the person and what is happening to us now.

OUR CONSCIENCE COMES TO THE RESCUE

They
heard the voice
of Being-Gods

As
that One
walked
in the garden
in the cool
of the day;

So,
the man
and
the woman
hid themselves
from the face
of Being-Gods
among the trees
of the Garden.

They heard the voice of Being-Gods: The person's conscience began to bother him.

As that one walked in the Garden in the cool of the day.

In the cool of the day: At the end of the enlightenment in the Garden. Night death is coming (the Dark Experience).

So the man and the woman hid from the face of Being-Gods among the trees of the Garden: So, the person began to eat of both Trees of Knowledge. Therefore, he lived for a time in light, and then, he chose to be darkness, which hid him in confusion from the person (face) of Being-Gods.

Jesus and Hiding from Ourselves.

We must be true to ourselves to live in the Garden; otherwise, we hide in darkness. Jesus speaks of that process of devolving into death in Saying 41 in *The Gospel of Thomas*:

He

Who
has
it
in his hand[1,2]

[1]*In his Hand:* In his control.

[2]*He who has it in his hand:* He who has control of his Garden Experience.

It
will be given
to him.[3]

[3]*It will be given to him:* More of the Garden Experience will be given to him (When one chooses the Soul Way, he will continue to use it to grow in the Garden Experience).

And
he

Who
has
not it
in his hand[4]

[4]*He who has not it in his hand:* He who does not possess the Garden Experience because he is in the Dark Experience...

The other
little bit

Which
has
he
in his hand

[5]*The other little bit which has he in his hand, it will be taken from him:* The other little bit of the Garden Experience which he controls will vanish. In each moment, we unconsciously or consciously either become more alive or dead.

It
will be taken
from him.[5]

BACK TO THE ALLEGORY

As described in this poem by Jesus, the person has chosen a "bit" of the Dark Experience by putting on garments made of fig leaves. Now we will watch to see as more bits of the Garden Experience are "taken from him" (Gen 3:9-10).

Being-Gods
called to the man
and said:

"Where
are
you?"

He
said:

"I
heard your voice
in the Garden

So
being afraid
and naked

I
hid."

Being-Gods called to the man and said: "Where are you?" Spirit asked a direct question to the masculine side of the person: "Where are you? In other words, Spirit asked, "Are you in the Light or Dark Experience?"

He said: "I heard your voice in the Garden, so being afraid and naked, I hid." I heard your voice in my conscience, so being afraid of my nakedness and not proud of it, I hid my real self from You behind a false, clothed self.

Now, Being-Gods continues the interrogation as we read in Gen 3:11:

And
Being-Gods
asked:

"Who
revealed your nakedness?

Did
you
eat of the tree

> *Of which*
> *I*
> *commanded you*
> *not to eat?"*

And Being-Gods asked: "Who revealed your nakedness? And Spirit asked, "Who showed you that you are perfect-as-is divine life?"

Did you eat of the Tree of which I commanded you not to eat?" Did you eat of the Tree of the Knowledge of Good and Bad?

The man's honest answer to both questions could honestly be something like: "Yes, I revealed my nakedness. Also, I ate of the Tree, of which you commanded me not to eat. Further, I am proud that I did those things because I now have evolved to be my real self with free choice. However, I used that ability to put on a garment and hide my divine self. I am sorry."

But as we will see in Gen 3:11, the person through his man side does not take responsibility for his actions:

> *The man*
> *said:*

> *"The woman*
> *you*
> *gave to me*

> *She*
> *gave me*
> *of the Tree*

> *And*
> *I*
> *ate it."*

The man said: "The woman you gave to me; she gave me of the Tree, and I ate it." Like a child who refuses to be responsible and face the consequences, the man said, "The woman persuaded me to eat the Dark Experience; therefore, she is responsible for revealing our nakedness. I am innocent." With that statement, the person hid even further from himself behind another lie. In that process, he committed another sin.

Having heard from the male side of the person, Judge Spirit now questions the woman in Gen 3:13. Let us see if she embraces her responsibility or hides.

Being-Gods
said to the woman:

"What
did
you
do?"

The woman
said:

"The snake
deceived me

And
I
ate it."

Being-Gods said to the woman: "What did you do?" Being-Gods asked a simple question, "What did you do?" To be real and remain in the Garden, she honestly could say, "I ate of the Tree of the Knowledge of Good and Bad." But, as we will see, she does not.

The woman said: "The snake deceived me, and I ate it." So, like the man, the woman decides not to take full responsibility for her choices, and instead, blames the snake. In that way, she chooses to sin by hiding, that is, by being less than entirely honest.

Summary

In this chapter, we see how our conscience calls us to go back into the Garden as soon as we have left it. We can retrace our steps by being honest with ourselves. When we are not, we hide our real selves behind layers of lies. Then, the "bit" of the Garden Experience that we had in our "hand" is taken from us.

The Soul Way

The Mind Way

Honestly monitor whether I am hiding my true identity.
↑
Live in automatic unconsciousness by not monitoring whether I am my true identity.

I am truth and light in the world.
↑
I am a dishonest, false god in the world.

CHAPTER EIGHT

THE GARDEN OF EDEN ALLEGORY: SPIRIT SENTENCES US

INTRODUCTION

The man and the woman admitted that they have eaten of the Dark Experience. However, instead of taking responsibility for their situation and discovering how to correct themselves in the future, they "hid" behind lies to themselves. We will now see how Spirit will punish everyone who sins and hides.

THE SNAKE'S PUNISHMENT

We read in Gen. 3:14 about what happens to the Snake as punishment for leading the woman to eat of the Tree of the Knowledge of Good and Bad.

Being-Gods
said to the snake:

"Because
you
did this

You
are
cursed
more than

every beast
and
more than
every living being
of the field,[10]

And
dust
you
will eat
all the days
of your life.

Being-Gods said to the snake: *"Because you did this."* Spirit said to our inner snake: "Because you tricked the woman into knowing the fruit of the Tree of the Knowledge of Good and Bad as perfect-as-is life.

You are cursed more than every beast and more than every living being of the field:

Every beast and every living being of the field. These are the animals that symbolize our abilities. For example, the lion often represents our courage.

To the snake: **"You are cursed more than every beast and living thing":** You will not inspire people to live more fully in the Garden Experience. Instead, you will inspire them to live in the Dark Experience.

And dust you will eat all the days of your life. Recall Gen. 2:7 "Being-Gods formed a person of the dust of the earth." "Dust of the earth" is a tiny bit of life-wisdom planted in reflective, receptive, consciousness. So, the snake will possess little wisdom as he inspires people to eat of the Tree of the Knowledge of Good and Bad.

---

[10] *Our current text inserts here: "On your belly you shall go." Because those words do not fit the structure, and because they do not make sense (was the snake hopping around on its tail before?), they were probably inserted by an early scribe.*

In Gen 3:15, Eve will now tell us why we will forever need to decide between living in or out of the Garden:

I

will put enmity
between the woman
and you
and
between her descendant
and your descendant;

Therefore
she
shall strike your head

And
you
shall strike her heel."

I will put enmity between the woman and you: I, Spirit, will make you, snake, the enemy of the woman. You, snake, will want the person to eat of the Tree of the Knowledge of Good and Bad, but she will want the person to eat of the Tree of the Knowledge of Life.

I will put enmity between her seed and your descendant: A "seed" is an insight. It can either inspire a person to choose to be more alive or dead. Therefore, Spirit will ensure that the snake's "seeds" conflict with the woman's.

Therefore, she shall strike your head: Therefore, the woman will stop you from leading.

And you shall strike her heel. And you, snake, shall use trickery to get her to do your bidding.

THE WOMAN'S PUNISHMENT

Spirit will spell out the fate of our woman in Gen 3:16:

To the woman
Being-Gods
said:

"I
will multiply greatly
your sorrow
in pregnancy,

In pain
you
shall bring forth children

Because
your desire
will be for the man
to rule you."

To the woman, Being-Gods said: "I will multiply your sorrow greatly in pregnancy: Spirit said to the woman, "When you consider unconditionally loving someone or something that you have called "bad," it will be a difficult struggle. For example, you will find it difficult to love an enemy unconditionally.

In pain you shall bring forth children: To our woman, Spirit said: "Every time you die to a false self to live your real child self, you will need to go through a painful birth process.

Because your desire will be for the man to rule you: You, woman, want the man to support you as you remove garments. He will not do that because he defends and promotes the person's ego. Therefore, you must develop the courage to become naked life against a world that will mock you.

Jesus and Our Painful Struggle to Give Birth to Ourselves.

Jesus may have been referring to this passage about the pain of giving birth to oneself when he composed Mark 8:35:

Whoever
is
the one

Who
is willing
to save his soul

[1] *Whoever is willing to save his soul will lose it:* Whoever will cling to his false self will lose his real self.

Will lose it.[1]

But
whoever
is
the one

Who
will destroy his soul

[2] *Whoever will destroy his soul... will save it.* Whoever will painfully destroy his ego, will gain his real self in the Garden.

Will save it.[2]

The Man's Punishment

Spirit has sentenced the snake and the woman. Let us see in Gen 3-17 what happens to our man:

To the man
Being-Gods
said:

"You
have listened
to the voice
of the woman

And
having eaten of the tree
of which
I
commanded
saying:

'Do
not eat of it.'

To the man, Being-Gods said: "You have listened to the voice of the woman." Spirit said to the man, you have listened to the woman rather than to me who told you not to eat of the Tree of the Knowledge of Good and Bad.

And you ate of the tree of which I commanded saying: 'Do not eat of it.' And you ate the Dark Experience.

Therefore,
of the cursed earth
you
will sorrowfully eat
all the days
of your life.

Because
it
will grow
thorns
and
thistles

And
you
shall eat of the herb
of the field,

And
in the sweat
of your face
you
will eat bread

Until
you
return to the earth;

For
you
are dust

And
you
will return to dust."[11,12]

Therefore, to the man, Being-Gods said, "Of the cursed earth sorrowfully eat all the days of your life because it will grow thorns and thistles.

Earth: our receptive, reflective consciousness.

Cursed earth: A receptive, reflective consciousness that has grown thorns and thistles (attachments to false selves).

---

[11] *Our current text inserts here Gen 3:20: "And the man called the woman's name 'Eve,' because she was the mother of all living beings." Because this sentence does not fit the structure, because it does not fit the Scene's theme which is punishment for disobeying, and because the man has already named her "woman" and not "Eve," it was probably inserted by a copyist. Thus, no one in the Garden of Eden Allegory is named Adam or Eve.*

[12] *Our current text inserts here Gen 3:21: "For the man and the woman Being-Gods made coats of skins and clothed them." Because this sentence does not fit the structure, and because the person was clothed earlier, this second clothing was probably inserted by a copyist.*

Therefore, to the man, Being-Gods said, "Of the cursed earth sorrowfully eat all the days of your life because it will grow thorns and thistles. To the man, Being Gods said, "You will eat (enjoy) the Dark Experience because the person will be attached primarily to people and things rather than to his soul, divine life.

And you shall eat of the herb of the field. And you, man, will eat of the herb of the field (the fruit of the Tree of the Knowledge of Good and Bad).

And in the sweat of your face, you will eat bread. And with great labor and sorrow, you will wean yourself off of eating the fruit of the Tree of the Knowledge of Good-Bad so that you and the person can eat the wisdom of the Tree of the Knowledge of Life.

Until you return to the earth: Until you and the person return to being completely fertile, receptive, reflective consciousness.

For you are dust. For Spirit made you and the person out of a bit of inspired, alive, receptive, reflective consciousness.

And you will return to dust. And your ultimate destiny is to return to being in the Garden with alive, receptive, reflective consciousness.

CHAPTER NINE

THE GARDEN OF EDEN ALLEGORY: SPIRIT BANISHES US

INTRODUCTION

Eve has shown that we all begin life in the Garden. We, then, put on garments and become false selves. To make matters worse, rather than take responsibility for being false, we hide behind layers of lies. Now in Gen 3:22-24, we will see what automatically happens to us.

WE GAIN OUR DIGNITY

Being-Gods
said:

"Behold,
the person
has become
one of us

Because
he
knows good and bad."

Being-Gods said, "Behold, the person has become one of us, knowing good and bad." Spirit said: Behold, the person has obtained both free choice and his dignity to be fully divine.

Jesus and Our Divinity

Jesus agrees with Eve that we are divine. Recall in *The Gospel of Thomas* (Saying 3b):

<table>
<tr><td>When
you
should know yourselves[1]</td><td>[1] *When you should know yourselves:* When you should know the real you...</td></tr>
<tr><td>Then
they
will know you[2]</td><td>[2] *Then, they will know you:* Then, people will see a radical difference in you.</td></tr>
<tr><td>And
you
will realize[3]</td><td>[3] *And you will realize:* And you will possess external confirmation.</td></tr>
<tr><td>That
you
are
sons
of the Father</td><td></td></tr>
<tr><td>Who
lives.[4]</td><td>[4] *That you are sons of the Father, who lives:* That you are divine sons and daughters of Spirit who lives in you.</td></tr>
</table>

According to Jesus, we cannot claim our dignity unless we know ourselves. When we do, we would see that we are divine light in the world.

Our Punishment

Let us read Gen 3:22-23 about what happens automatically when we eat of the Tree of the Knowledge of Good and Bad:

And now,
lest
the person
put forth his hand,
to take of the Tree
of Life

And
eat

And
live forever,

Being-Gods
sent him forth
from the Garden of Eden
to till the earth

From which
he
was taken.

And now, lest the person put forth his hand and take of the Tree of Life, and eat, and live forever:

Lest the person put forth his hand: Lest the person easily takes control…

To **"take"** is to choose.

Live forever: Live divine, eternal life.

And now, lest the person put forth his hand and take of the Tree of Life and eat and live forever: And now, to prevent someone from being in the Garden at the same time that he is in darkness…

Being-Gods sent him forth from the Garden of Eden to work the earth. Therefore, a natural law within us sends us "forth from the Garden" as soon as we put on garments (false selves).

When one finds himself in the Dark Experience, and he wants to be back in the Garden, he must identify how he has put on garments and how he will become naked. Then, he must implement his insights. That process is called "working" one's "earth."

Buddha and Eternal Life

In two poems, Buddha also tells us that we can know that we are eternal life:

Cross over
to the other shore[1]

And
live beyond life
and death.[2]
(Ch.24)

[1]*Cross over to the other shore:* Cross over your river of passions to the Garden.

[2]*And live beyond life and death:* And live the eternal you.

Buddha calls the "world" the land on this side of the river of passions. The land of freedom and light is on the other side (his disciples will, after his death, call the other side of the river, "Nirvana.") Only on the other side can one "live beyond life and death," that is, live in the eternal now.

Buddha (Ch. 2) spoke of the "work" we do to become eternally alive on the other side of the river:

The fool
sleeps
as
one
dead.

But
the master
is awake

And
he
lives eternally.

So
wake up
reflect
notice
and
work earnestly
and carefully.

Live on the Way
(of the Soul)

And
the light
will increase in you.

The master
who
guards his mind
and
fears confusion
discovers his Way
to stillness.

By paying attention,
the master
transforms himself
into an island

Which
the river of passions
cannot conquer.

The fool sleeps as one dead. The fool does not pay attention to the signals that tell him that he is in the Dark Experience. For example, a fool is not alarmed that he lives in the past or future, or that he is filled with regret and worry. None of these feelings and thoughts become conscious in him because he is so unconsciously dead in darkness on this side of the river of passions.

The master who safeguards his mind and fears confusion has found his Way to stillness. The master watches his thoughts and feelings. He does not live on automatic. He dreads confusing the Garden with the Dark Experience.

The master is awake, and he lives eternally. The person in the Garden does not live in the past or future. He lives in an eternal now.

Live on the Way (of the Soul), and the light will increase in you: This is the guarantee of Eve, Abraham, Buddha, and Jesus. The opposite is also true: Live on the Way of the Mind, and the darkness will increase in you.

By paying attention and working, the master transforms himself into an island which the river of passions cannot overwhelm. By mastering his conscious feelings and thoughts on the Soul Way, the master gains the wisdom to protect himself from the flood of dark emotions that could otherwise overwhelm him.

OUR AUTOMATIC PUNISHMENT

As soon as we choose to be in darkness, we are automatically banished to a world of suffering (Genesis 3:24):

So
Being-Gods
drove out the person

And
placed at the east
of the Garden
of Eden
a Cherubim
and
a flaming sword

Which
turned around
to guard the Way
to the Tree of Life.

So, Being-Gods drove out the person.

As soon as we put on clothes (false selves), we immediately drive ourselves out of the Garden and into darkness. (Later, in Genesis 4:11, we learn that when one leaves the Garden, the land of darkness is called, "Nod," which means, a "World of Wandering").

And Spirit placed to the East of the Garden a Cherubim:

The East: The sun is a symbol of light inspiration in the Garden. It rises in the East to guide a person into the Garden.

Cherubim: An angel. It is the voice of Spirit that inspires us to eat the fruit of the Tree of the Knowledge of Life. Therefore, each of us possesses both a snake telling him to enjoy death as life and an angel that tells him to avoid darkness and live a divine life.

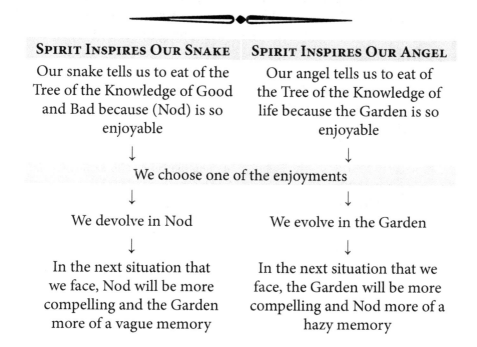

SPIRIT INSPIRES OUR SNAKE	SPIRIT INSPIRES OUR ANGEL
Our snake tells us to eat of the Tree of the Knowledge of Good and Bad because (Nod) is so enjoyable	Our angel tells us to eat of the Tree of the Knowledge of life because the Garden is so enjoyable
↓	↓
We choose one of the enjoyments	
↓	↓
We devolve in Nod	We evolve in the Garden
↓	↓
In the next situation that we face, Nod will be more compelling and the Garden more of a vague memory	In the next situation that we face, the Garden will be more compelling and Nod more of a hazy memory

BACK TO THE ALLEGORY

And Spirit placed to the east of the Garden a Cherubim and a flaming sword which turned around to guard the Way to the Tree of Life.

A sword: The natural law that demands that we cut off our false selves to enter the Garden.

A flaming sword: The sword consists of flaming love for us, not cold hate.

The **sword which turns around:** It "turns around" to guard the Garden from all of the false ways we may try to use to get into it. Those methods include taking drugs, buying things, indulging in distractions, etc. The sword sees our games and refuses to let us get into the Garden.

JESUS AS THE SWORD

The "sword" is a principle of our being. It tells us the difference between false and real life. The sword can also be another person who lives on the Soul Way. He sees our games and does not support them.

In *The Gospel of Mark,* the author describes Jesus as a sword which turns around to divide dead people from those who are alive (Mk 3:34):

<table>
<tr>
<td>

And
his mother
and his brothers
came[1]

</td>
<td>

[1]*And his mother and his brothers came:* And his mother and his brothers, who identified with their religious faith and not their naked selves, came.

</td>
</tr>
<tr>
<td>

And
they
stood outside[2]

</td>
<td>

[2]*And they stood outside:* And they stood on the death Torah principles in Nod.

</td>
</tr>
</table>

And
they
sent unto him,
calling him.[3]

And
a crowd
was sitting
about him

And
they
chattered:

"Behold your mother
and your brothers
outside

And
they
are seeking you."[4]

And
Jesus
answered them
by saying:

"Who
are
my mother
and my brothers?"[5]

And
having looked around[6]
on the ones
about him
sitting
in a circle
he said:

[3]*And they sent into him, calling him:* And Jesus' family, because they did not want to contaminate themselves with his Soul Way, asked him to join their Mind Way in Judaism.

[4]*Behold your mother and your brothers outside, and they are seeking you.* This sentence is irony. Jesus' mother and brothers are not seeking him and his Way. Instead, they want to convert him to live in their mental darkness.

[5]*Who are my mother and my brothers?* With this question, Jesus becomes the "sword" challenging convention that says that he should identify with his family and their traditions.

[6]*And having looked around...he said:* And being the "sword" that "turned around to guard the Way to the Tree of the Knowledge of Life," he said:

"Behold my mother
and my brothers!

The one
having done the will
of God
is
my brother
and sister
and mother."[7]

[7]*He said: "Behold my mother and brothers, the one having done the will of God is my brother, and sister, and mother:"* He said, "Look at those around me on the Soul Way doing the will of God. They do not identify with their birth family, their religion, nor their traditions. They are led only by Spirit. People like them are my true family."

I show in my book, *The Semitic Secret* that the Gospel of Mark is a historical allegory. Consequently, the figure of Jesus is a stand-in for a person on the Soul Way. So, Jesus and we, to the degree that we are on the Soul Way, also are the swords that "turn around" to guard the way to the Tree of Life.

In *The Gospel of Thomas* (Saying 16), Jesus explains in another powerful poem how he and others on the Soul Way can be swords:

Perhaps
they
are thinking

Namely
men[1]

That
I
have come
to throw peace
upon the world;[2]

And
they
know
not

That
I
have come
to throw divisions
upon the earth:[3]

[1]*Men:* Dead men on the Mind Way.

[2]*To throw peace upon the world:* To speak comforting words to dark, dead men.

[3]*To throw divisions upon the earth:* To cause divisions within us when we try to live on the two Ways at the same time.

Fire[4]
sword[5]
and
war.[6]

[4]*Fire:* Words that confront.

[5]*Sword:* Words and actions that expose the difference between our false selves and real selves.

[6]*War:* Words that cause a person's real self to fight his false self. Words that will cause division between those on the Mind Way and those on the Soul Way.

Jesus and his followers "throw divisions" in the world by preaching the difference between the Soul and Mind Ways.

THE SOUL WAY

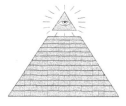

THE MIND WAY

These people bring fire, sword, and war to the Mind Way "world."

↑

These people bring compromise, conformity, accommodation, tolerance, and false peace to the Mind Way "world."

GARDEN OF EDEN SUMMARY

Eve has created an around-the-fire bedtime Allegory for children and adults. It is humorous, dramatic, and enjoyable to hear and read. It is a self-help guide for all of us. Its central theme: we were born whole and divine in the Garden, but society inevitably seduces us to live in Nod. Our goal in life, then, is to return to the Garden in ever more profound ways. Jesus says this in *The Gospel of Thomas* (Saying 49):

Those blest ones[1]

They
are
the single ones[2]

[1]*Blest ones:* Those in oneness with who they are, with the core life in others, and with Spirit.

[2]*Single ones:* People congruent with their real selves.

and
the chosen ones;³

For
you
will discover the
Kingdom⁴

For
you
are out
of it⁵

And again
you
will be going
there.⁶

³*Chosen ones:* People who have been given life.

⁴*For you will discover the kingdom:* For you will rediscover the Garden.

⁵*For you are out of it:* For you were born in the Garden.

⁶*And again, you will be going there.* And again, you blessed ones will be returning to the fulfilled life you lived as a child.

THE SOUL WAY

THE MIND WAY

Garden of Eden.

↑

Nod (the Land of Wandering).

Takes of the Tree of Life and lives forever.

↑

Takes of the Tree of Death and dies forever (until he chooses life).

CHAPTER TEN

THE ABRAHAM ALLEGORY: THE COVENANT

INTRODUCTION

The ancients all over the world understood that the Garden of Eden Allegory contained the secrets to being fulfilled no matter how difficult things were in their lives. Consequently, Abraham, Buddha, and Jesus wanted to explain how to live in the Garden all day, every day.

THE COVENANT

As noted earlier, we call the author of the Abraham saga, the fourth major story in Genesis, "Abraham,"[13] but we do not know the true identity of the Allegory's composer.

Abraham was born in Ur, which was in Southern Iraq. One day, His father, Terah, took him, his wife Sara, and many of his relatives to Haran, a city in Upper Mesopotamia whose site is near the modern village of Altınbaşak, Turkey. While there, Spirit presented Abraham with a contract, which also is called a "Covenant" (Genesis 12:1-5):

---

[13] *Abraham: His birth name was Abram, which means "high father." In Gen. 17:5 we read that Being-Gods changes his name to "Abraham," which means "father of a multitude."*

*Being
said to Abraham:*

*Go from the land
of your tribe
and
your father's house*

*And
go to the earth*

*That
I
will show you,*

*And
I
will make you
into a great people.*

*And
I
will bless you*

*And
I
will magnify your name
greatly*

*And
you
will be a blessing.*

*And
I
will bless those*

The ones

Who
bless you;

And
I
will curse those

The ones
Who
curse you."

Spirit's Covenant contains two parts: First, a command, and second, a promise of the reward that will be given to Abraham, and through him to those that fulfill the directive.

The Covenant is introduced by the phrase "Being said to Abraham." That phrase tells us that we are reading an allegory. We know that because history texts describe physical facts, not a God talking to a person.

When a history writer wants to tell us that Spirit inspired someone like Napoleon, he will establish a setting to let us know that. For example, he might say, "Napoleon left his tent, went apart from his men, and waited to be inspired about how to arrange his troops."

We are not introduced to Spirit talking to Abraham in that way. Instead, we see the same abrupt entrance of Spirit that we saw in the Garden Allegory. That is an indication that we are reading an allegory.

We have no evidence that Abraham lived. So, more likely, we are reading a pure allegory—one some unknown wise person composed to explain how each of us might use our angel to get by our sword to live in the Garden all day, every day.

Analysis of the Covenant

Being said to Abraham: "Go from the land of your tribe and your father's house and go to the earth that I will show you."

Our current Hebrew text reads: **"Go from the land ('erets) of your tribe…and go to the land ('erets) that I will show you."**

As I explained previously, 'erets (land) means, metaphorically, unreceptive, unreflective consciousness. So, we surmise that Spirit is not going to lead Abraham out of darkness into more of the same. That makes no sense. Therefore, the original text must have stated that Spirit will lead Abraham out of 'erets "land" and into "adamah" (earth)—receptive, reflective, consciousness, which is necessary for him to be in the Garden.

There are also structural reasons to believe that a copyist changed "adamah" to "'erets." I explain those reasons in my Book, *The Semitic Secret.*

So, the original text almost certainly was: **"Go from the _land_ ('erets) of your tribe…and go to the _earth_ (adama) that I will show you."**

That I will show you: Spirit tells Abraham: "Because you do not know how to leave the Dark Experience to be in the Light Experience, I must 'show you.'" As we will see, Spirit does that by leading Abraham on the Soul Way.

Promised Earth

Because the original text became corrupted, people today think of Abraham as going to the "Promised Land," a physical territory. However, he is going to the "Promised Earth," which is the Garden of Eden (the Light Experience).

EXERCISE

A question for reflection: "Go from the land of your tribes and your Father's house" means? (Put "yes" or "no" after each of the following options):

1. Go from Nod.

2. Go from the Dark Experience of your tribes and your family.

3. Go from the beliefs of your tribe (neighborhood, nation, etc.) and your family.

4. Go from the false identities of your tribe and your family.

5. Go from the dis-empowering control of others.

6. Go from being unconscious.

7. Go from your false selves.

My answer: "Yes" to all of the above options.

EXERCISE:

A Question for Reflection: "Go to the earth" means? (Put "yes" or "no" after each of the following options):

1. Go to the Light Experience.

2. Go to being naked.

3. Go to being wise-love of all.

4. Go to mental/spiritual health.

5. Go to being yourself.

6. Go to being conscious.

7. Go to being fulfilled.

8. Go to being one with your core self and the core selves of others.

My answer: "Yes" to all of the above options.

EXERCISE:

A Question for Reflection: Was the Covenant offered only to Abraham or is it also offered to each of us today?

MY ANSWER:

The Command, "Go from the land of your tribe and your father's house and go to the earth that I will show you," is one with our being. It shouts, "Be you!" When we are conscious, we hear it. When we are unconscious in our "land," we do not hear or follow the command. As a result, we are banished from the Promised Earth and suffer in our Dark Land.

We are learning about two commands that are natural laws in our being: the Garden Command and the Covenant. Unless we follow them, we will never have a fulfilled life.

And
I
will make you
into a great people.

And
I
will bless you

And
I
will magnify your name
greatly

And

you

will be a blessing.

And I will make you into a great people: And I, Spirit, will make you and all who follow your Soul Way into a great, united people.

And I will bless you: And as you grow, you will become more the divine, fulfilled life that you are.

And I will magnify your name greatly: And I will make you a more influential person in the world.

And you will be a blessing: And everyone will recognize Me and my life in you.

And

I

will bless those

The ones

Who

bless you;

And

I

will curse those

The ones

Who

curse you.

I will bless those, the ones who bless you: I will provide more "life" to those who observe and respect divine life in you.

I will curse those, the ones who curse you: I will remove "life" from those who denigrate the divine life in you.

Jesus explains how one is cursed and blessed in his marvelous "Lion Poem" in *The Gospel of Thomas* (Saying 7):

A blessed one[1]

He
is
the lion[2]

The one

That
the man[3]
will eat[4]

And
the lion
comes to be
the man.[5]

And
he
is cursed[6]

Namely
the man[7]

The one

That
the lion
will eat[8]

And
the lion
comes to be
the man.[9]

[1] *A blessed one:* One who is in oneness with Spirit.

[2] *Lion:* A highly-evolved, powerful, wise person who is walking on the Soul Way.

[3] *Man:* A dead man who has become a seeker of the life and wisdom of the lion.

[4] *He is the lion, the one that the man will eat:* He is the light leader who speaks the wisdom that the seeker takes in and digests.

[5] *And the Lion comes to be the man:* And the spirit of the lion becomes the spirit of the seeker.

[6] *And he is cursed:* And he is made miserable as he walks on the Mind Way.

[7] *Man:* A dead person who chooses not to learn from the wise, light lion.

[8] *The one that the lion will eat:* The unconscious, dead man that the lion attacks with his "sword."

[9] *And the lion comes to be the man:* And the wise, loving leader comes to be the nightmare that haunts the terrified man on the Mind Way.

Let us apply Jesus' understanding to the Covenant:

And
I
will bless those

The ones

Who
bless you;[1]

[1]*I will bless those, the ones who bless you.* I, Spirit, will fill with divine "life" those who learn from you.

And
I
will curse those

The ones

Who
curse you.[2]

[2]*And I will curse those, the ones who curse you.* I, Spirit, will banish those into the Dark Experience who do not learn from you how to live on the Soul Way.

JESUS TEACHES HOW TO RECOGNIZE A BLESSED PERSON

The Covenant reads: **"And you will be a blessing."** In *The Gospel of Thomas* (Saying 15), Jesus tells of us how we can recognize one who is blessed.

When
you
should peer upon
he[1]

[1]*When you should peer upon he:* When you should see with your third-eye a person who lives the Garden Command and the Covenant...

Who
was
not begotten
inward
out of a woman[2]

[2]*He who was not begotten inward out of a woman:* He who is a divine being that a physical body could not produce.

Prostrate
yourselves
onto your face;[3]

[3]*Prostrate yourself on your face:* Humble yourself.

And
there
worship him;[4]

[4]*Worship him:* Venerate the divine life that is in that person.

He who is there	
He is your Father.⁵	⁵*He who is there, he is your Father:* He whom you experience in that person is Spirit.

Jesus experienced that everyone, to the degree that he lives on the Soul Way, is, like him, the son or daughter of God. In that way, each of us can be a "blessing" to everyone else.

EXERCISE:

Question for Reflection: Have you ever seen Spirit?

My answer: Everyone may see Spirit in a newborn child, in an adult who lives naked (i.e., without pretenses), that is, who wise-loves everyone else as their soul brother and sister. But some (including me) sometimes do not "peer" at one of those marvels in front of us with an inspired, single-eye, and recognize the divine presence of Spirit.

SUMMARY

Spirit told Abraham and us that to be fulfilled, we must "go" from the control of our tribes (culture) and our family and "go" independently with Spirit guidance into the Promised Earth.

Jesus teaches how we "go" to the "Promised Earth" in *The Gospel of Thomas* (Saying 111):

Whoever is the one Who discovers himself on his own¹	¹*Whoever is the one who discovers himself on his own:* Whoever goes from the land (expectations) of his tribes (relatives, neighborhood, religion, nation) and his father's house (the traditions and values of his family) and goes independently into the Promised Earth (Light Experience), he will become a person who…

The world
is
worthy of him
not.[2]

[2] *The world is worthy of him, not:*
The dark ones will not be worthy of sharing his life.

Jesus tells us in this poem, that unless we challenge everything we have been taught that we are, and unless we make everyone else's opinions of ourselves secondary to our own, we will forever live in the "land" of the Dark Experience.

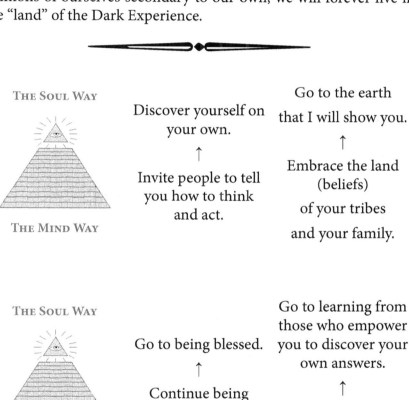

THE SOUL WAY

Discover yourself on your own.
↑
Invite people to tell you how to think and act.

THE MIND WAY

Go to the earth that I will show you.
↑
Embrace the land (beliefs) of your tribes and your family.

THE SOUL WAY

Go to being blessed.
↑
Continue being cursed.

THE MIND WAY

Go to learning from those who empower you to discover your own answers.
↑
Remain bound to the ideas of indoctrinators.

CHAPTER ELEVEN

THE ABRAHAM ALLEGORY: OUR GUIDE

INTRODUCTION

Being has said:

Go to the earth

That
I
will show you,

Which means:

Go to the Light Experience

That
I
will show you
because
you alone
do not know the Way.

The Covenant is a natural law that exists in our being. We become aware of it with our third-eye. In essence, it is a promise that if we become like Abraham, empty of all of our previous attachments to things, people, and their associated dogmas, we will be able to communicate directly with Spirit. Spirit will, then, guide us to live in the Promised Earth (the "Garden," "Nirvana," and the "Kingdom").

THE FIRST REASON WE NEED SPIRIT GUIDANCE

We did not leave the womb and begin crawling around, asking, "What official religious and secular dogmas do I need to believe to be a valued person?" As babes, we knew we were perfect-as-is and so we began happily to discover our answers on our own.

Then, our family and friends, teachers and clergy, and the authors of scripture books, our therapists, the media, etc. interrupted our natural development and, following their Mind Way conditioning, said, in essence, "Oh no, you are not perfect-as-is. You need to memorize, believe, and live our artificial dogmas. Then, you will be like us, perfect, saved, and good in the Promised Earth."

That is a lie. Look at the evidence: If adults knew how to enter the Promised Earth, we would all be there. But around every corner, all we see is conflict. Most of the global community lives in Nod, the state of wandering on the Mind Way.

A small child experiences the Promised Earth. He also senses that all adults, to some degree, guide him into the Dark Experience. That is why most children demand to be independent.

Who will help the child to guard himself against indoctrinating adults and instead empower him and guide him to discover his answers for growing in the Light Experience?

The child's guide must be someone who wise-loves the child unconditionally. That guide must know his limitations, strengths, and his unique purpose, history, physical health, needs, dreams, and all of the laws in his being (such as the Garden Command and the Covenant). The child's perfect guide, therefore, is Spirit.

THE SECOND REASON WE NEED SPIRIT'S GUIDANCE

The short answer: We need Spirit to show us higher levels of truth. All of us could live higher levels of truth.

Jesus and Levels of Truth

Jesus explains that truth has levels, that is, that it is 3D. He says that in *The Gospel of Thomas*, Chapter 3, Poem 2 (Saying 11a):

This heaven[1]

It
will pass away;[2]

And
the one
above it

It
will pass away.[3]

And
those

Who
are
dead

They
live
not.[4]

And
those

Who
live

They
will die
not.[5]

[1]*Heaven:* A level of truth and wise-love about oneself, others, and the world.

[2]*Pass away:* Our present view of truth and wise-love will change as we become more our real selves.

[3]*And the one above it, it will pass away.* As we continue to evolve, each of our higher levels of truth and wise-love also will pass away.

[4]*And those who are dead, they will live not:* Those who live a lower level of truth and wise-love will be in eternal darkness until they change. Unless they evolve, they will never be living a full life.

[5]*And those who live, they will die not:* And those who live at a high level of truth and wise-love will not be eternally miserable in the dark experience.

In this poem, Jesus states that the pursuit of truth is 3D. There are higher and lower levels of personal truth about all things. Those living high in the Light Experience know the truth of themselves, others, and how to solve problems one way. Those living low in the Dark Experience know reality very differently. Graphically:

HIGHER TRUTHS

LOWER TRUTHS

For example, Hitler knew the truth about Jews and other, so-called, imperfect humans. Eve, Abraham, Buddha, and Jesus also knew the truth about everyone. One person knew low life truths, the others, higher life truths. As we grow on the Soul Way, we know truer truths and manifest higher levels of love.

Single-eye intuition can reveal high truths. Two-eye reasoning can only reveal low-level truths.

Spirit, one with our soul, reveals higher level, personal truths through our intuition. No theologian, philosopher, therapist, or another guru can teach high levels of truth and love. These people can suggest higher levels, but only Spirit can confirm their insights to an individual.

HIGHER TRUTHS

LOWER TRUTHS

Truth is different for everyone depending on each person's level of wise-love of all. If we intuit ever-higher truths, we will live more fully in the Promised Earth.

HIGHER TRUTHS

LOWER TRUTHS

A person on the Soul Way continually suspends his current level of beliefs to intuit and live higher truths.

↑

A person on the Mind Way maintains his current levels of beliefs and never evolves.

HIGHER TRUTHS

LOWER TRUTHS

To the degree that people live on different levels of truth, to that degree, they will never fully agree.

HIGHER TRUTHS

LOWER TRUTHS

Humanity will never evolve to solve its problems unless leaders live a high level of truth and wise-love.

Conclusion: Abraham is correct. We cannot get into the Promised Earth individually or as a global community unless Spirit guides us to high levels of truth and wise-love.

Exercise:

Questions for Reflection: Consider five leaders: Eve, Abraham, Buddha, Jesus, and Hitler.

1. Which of them see the true nature of another person?

2. Which of them are best able to wisely love another?

3. Which of them can best be both generous to another and, at the same time, hold the other accountable for how they use the generosity?

4. Which of them would best evaluate the situation objectively before planning or intervening?

5. Which of them would be the best president of a company or a country?

6. Which of them would be the best parent?

My answer to all of the questions: The person who has both the most experience and expertise in the matters, and who lives the highest level of truth and love.

Our Third-Ear

Our intuitive soul-knowing can also be represented by a single-third-ear.

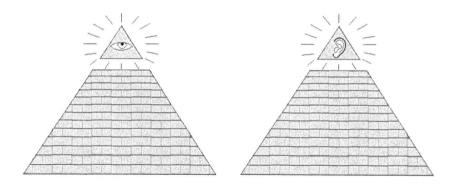

Jesus and Our Third Ear

Jesus used the "third-ear" metaphor for intuitive knowing. For example, a *core* principle of Jesus' teachings is in the following poem:

He[1]

Who
has
his ear[2]
to listen[3]

Let him
listen.[4]

[1]*He:* He who wants to evolve to a higher level of truth and –love…

[2]*Ear:* Third, single, intuitive ear.

[3]*To listen:* To listen to Spirit.

[4]*Let him listen:* Let him be supported in his listening.

We find this poem *twelve* times in both the New Testament and in *The Gospel of Thomas*. None of Jesus' other parables or sayings are quoted more than four times. Consequently, *we deduce that third-ear listening to Spirit was the <u>foundation</u> of his gospel.*

Mental Reasoning vs. Soul Revealing

We can get our personal answers through mental reasoning or soul revealing. To do the latter, we use our third-eye and ear. Jesus explains the revealing process in *The Gospel of Thomas* (Saying 8a):

A man
is comparable
to a fisherman
wise,[1]

The one

Who
threw his net
into the sea.[2]

And
he
conveyed it up
from the sea

[1]*A man is comparable to a fisherman wise.* A seeker who desires to communicate with Spirit is like a person who has mastered himself and the skills necessary to catch an elusive quarry.

[2]*The seeker who threw his net into the sea:* The seeker who revealed information welling up from his soul-sea of deep emotions. (He does not *reason* to ideas, he *reveals* or *senses* them, as does an artist or creative person).

It
full of fish[3]

Little ones
from below[4]

And
among them

He
discovered a great fish.[5]

The good man

Namely
the fisherman
wise,

Threw the little ones

All of those fish

Back down
into the sea.[6]

And
he
chose the great fish
without trouble.[7]

[3]*Fish:* Soul ideas and impressions.

[4]*Little ones from below:* Less important ones from his soul.

[5]*A Great fish:* An important insight that confronted him with his flaws and helped him to evolve in truth and love.

[6]*Threw the little ones back down into the sea:* Consigned the less critical insights back to semi-consciousness.

[7]*He chose the great fish without trouble:* He did not shy away from the problem caused by an idea that both confronts his inadequacies and gives him a vision of how he might evolve.

In this parable, Jesus describes a process that one may use to obtain insights from Spirit. First, one goes apart to an environment where he can fish for ideas. Second, he becomes still and let ideas flow up to him from the soul "below." Then, he sorts through these ideas, seeking the one that will transform him. When he has found that insight, he easily gives up his former beliefs to embrace the new, revolutionary belief *tentatively*. (On the soul way, most beliefs are "tentative" because they will be given up to live higher ones).

The fisherman (seeker) does not reason his way to a "big fish" at a higher level of truth and love. Rather, he empties himself of his former beliefs in order for Spirit to *reveal* what he needs to know.

Buddha (Ch. 5) was a leader who taught people to reveal their truths:

The fool[1]
is
careless,

[1] *The fool*: The person on the Mind Way.

But
the master[2]
attends to his watching[3]
as
his most precious treasure.

[2] *The master*: The person on the Soul Way.

[3] *Attends to his watching*: Organizes his life so that he can possess the stillness necessary to notice the information bubbling up from his soul.

[4] *He contemplates*: He reflects on the new information, especially that which teaches him how he can leave his former ways of believing and acting to live at a higher level of truth and love.

He
contemplates[4]

And
he
discovers true joy.[5]

[5] *He discovers true joy*: He discovers the Promised Earth.

Eve, Abraham, Buddha, and Jesus never encourage people to "reason to" or "deduce" primarily their personal answers. They also never say to "believe" in the dogmatic answers of others. Instead, they teach people how to third eye and ear "discover" and "reveal" higher levels of truth and wise-love.

THE REQUIREMENTS FOR THIRD-EYE AND EAR KNOWING

Why do we **not** use our intuition primarily to get the information we need? In *The Gospel of Thomas* (Saying 19a), Jesus provides one answer: To communicate with Spirit, we must be in-the-moment.

A blessed one
is
he

[1] *A blessed one is he who will come to be from the beginning*: An individual who is in oneness with Spirit will be in-the-present with what is.

Who
will come to be
from the beginning[1]

Before he comes to be.[2]	[2]*Before he comes to be:* Before he takes the first thought or step to do anything else.

To communicate with Spirit, Jesus teaches that one must be in the present. There, one can use his single-eye and ear intuition to both listen to and speak to Spirit. When we are living mentally in the past or future, we are on the Mind Way, reasoning with our two eyes and two ears.

We learned earlier that one cannot be in the present unless he embraces all that is as perfect-as-is life. However, Jesus found that one cannot do that without Spirit inspiration. Therefore, when we find ourselves in the Dark Experience, he counsels us to go apart, open to let go of any attachments to interpreting things as "bad and good," and then, wait for the insight that teaches us how to be in the moment. Once there, we may gain the insights necessary to think and act at a high level of truth and love.

Jesus tells us that there is an additional benefit to living in the "beginning" (*The Gospel of Thomas*, Poem 18b):

A blessed one is he Who will stand on his feet in the beginning[1]	[1]*A blessed one is he who will stand on his feet in the beginning:* A person "blessed" because he lives the Covenant is he who will be strong and firm in the "now moment."
And he will know the end[2]	[2]*And he will know the end:* The end is the same as the beginning—stillness and joy in the "now" Promised Earth.
And he will take a taste not of death.[3]	[3]*And He will take a taste not of death:* And he will obtain the insights to not be at all in the Dark Experience.

According to Jesus, our beginning is our end. If we live in the past or future, every idea that comes to us eventually will lead us further into living in past regret or future worry. If we live in the present; however, Spirit will provide the insights to live that way forever.

THE SOUL WAY

THE MIND WAY

Be stillness in motion in the present (in the beginning).
↑
Be all motion in the past or future.

Continually be a fisherman for higher insights.
↑
Be satisfied with one's present level of development.

CHAPTER TWELVE

THE ABRAHAM ALLEGORY: CIRCUMCISE YOURSELF

In the Abraham Allegory, the author introduces us to a circumcision ritual that metaphorically expresses a commitment to living the Covenant (Genesis 17:1, 11-12):

> *Being said to Abraham, "You shall circumcise the flesh of your foreskin, and it will be a sign of the Covenant between you and me. And he that is eight days old shall be circumcised, every male child."*

Being said to Abraham, "You shall circumcise the flesh of your foreskin, and it will be a sign of the Covenant between you and me."

When one is circumcised, a piece of useless, bacteria-holding flesh is cut from an organ that can express unconditional wise-love. When one chooses to follow the Covenant, one is to "go" from useless cultural indoctrinators and their disease-causing beliefs to "go" to the Promised Earth as guided by Spirit. Thus, an act of "circumcision" is a metaphor for the Covenant Command. Here it is again:

> *Being*
> *said to Abraham:*
>
> *"Go from the land*
> *of your tribes*
> *and*
> *your father's house*

And

go to the earth

That
I
will show you,

And
I
will make you
into a great people.

And
I
will bless you

And
I
will magnify your name
greatly

And
you
will be a blessing."

Go from the land of your tribes and your father's house. Circumcise yourself from the brainwashing of your culture and your family. Or, circumcise yourself from your former truths in which you find your security. Or, circumcise yourself of the sick, Mind Way. Or, circumcise yourself of the slavery of theological and secular religions to be free to live your own answers with the guidance of Spirit in the Promised Earth.

In Genesis 17:1-12, circumcision is presented as a physical act. But physical circumcision is not the primary meaning of these verses. It is a metaphor for a psychological/spiritual growth process, just like the act of taking off a garment in the Garden Allegory. If one does it physically, it is a "sign" of dedication to the Covenant, and most importantly, to Spirit guidance.

When we are in the Promised Earth, we do not need to circumcise ourselves figuratively. There, we are naked of garments (false selves).

And he that is eight days old shall be circumcised, every male child.

Seven days old: The number "seven" symbolizes perfection. When one is seven days old, he is perfect-as-is in his enlightened "days."

Eight days old: The number "eight" symbolizes the imperfection that happens to a person when he puts on garments. A child is born seven days old and is taught by his parents and his culture to be eight days old.

Child: At our core, we are all naked children. We stop being that when we identify with our false selves and their implied beliefs.

When a person identifies with his false selves, He lives imperfect, unenlightened, on the 8th day. It is then that he needs circumcision, the removal of his false selves.

Every male. Every person has a male and female side. It is the male side that needs to be circumcised when it has led one to put on clothes to be "good" and to condemn others who differ, as "bad." Our male side is the one who chooses to listen to the snake. Our women listens to our angel speaking Spirit's messages.

To be clear, every woman has a male side that needs to be circumcised when she lives in the Dark Experience. Therefore, circumcision is for everyone.

And he that is eight days old shall be circumcised, every male child. And he that has taken on a false self and a dedication to a false-god indoctrinator shall be circumcised, every male side of every man and *woman*.

Jesus, Buddha, and Circumcision

Jesus explains the true meaning of circumcision in *The Gospel of Thomas* (Saying 53):

His disciples
asked Jesus
this:

"Circumcision[1]

It
is
beneficial
or
not to us?"

[1]*Circumcision:* Physically removing the old and useless.

He
said to them
this:
"If
it
were beneficial

Their Father
would beget them
out of their mothers
circumcised.[2]

[2]*If it were beneficial, their father would beget them out of their mothers circumcised:* If physical circumcision were useful, the laws of nature would implement it.

Rather
circumcision
true in spirit[3]
has found merit

[3]*Circumcision true in spirit:* The removal of our clothes (false identities) and the detachment from false-god indoctrinators is the true spirit of circumcision.

All of it.

Jesus did not teach or engage in the ritual of physical circumcision. He taught the true meaning of that ritual when he explained how to become naked.

Buddha (Ch. 7) also wrote a poem that describes the act of spiritual circumcision:

The master[1]

surrenders his beliefs;[2]

[1]*The master:* The person who both has become a king or queen over himself and his interactions and has chosen the Promised Earth as his goal...

[2]*Surrenders his beliefs:* Suspends his beliefs at his present level of truth to develop higher-level beliefs.

And, therefore, peers beyond the end and the beginning.[3]

[3]*And, therefore, peers beyond the end and the beginning.* And thus, the master becomes in the eternal now (the Light Experience).

He cuts all dependencies[4]

[4]*He cuts all dependencies:* He goes (circumcises himself) from his relationships with his indoctrinating leaders and their dogmas.

And he surrenders all desires[5] to rise.[6]

[5]*He surrenders all desires:* He circumcises himself from his wishes to live on the Mind Way.

[6]*To rise:* To evolve in life in the Promised Earth.

Circumcision (to "go from the land...") is a painful procedure, so most of us try to be on both the Mind and Soul Way. In *The Gospel of Thomas* (Saying 47) Jesus explains that neither Abraham nor we can serve both Spirit and an indoctrinating, disempowering voice (such as sometimes heard from a parent, a theologian, a professor, an esteemed leader, a media personality, or a peer) and get into the Promised Earth.

In no way

Can a man climb onto horses two[1,2]

[1]*Horses two:* A horse represents power. Within us are two powers; our light self and the group of dark, ego selves that we create.

[2]*In no way can a man climb onto horses two:* In no way can a person use the power inherent in both the Mind and Soul Way.

And
he
stretch bows two.[3]

In no way
can
a servant
serve lords two[4]

Or
he
will honor the one

And the other one
he
will despise.

No man
drinks wine
old

And immediately
he
desires
to drink wine
new.[5]
And
they
do
not pour wine
new
into wineskins
old

So that
they
are not split open.[6]

[3]*In no way can a person stretch bows two:* A bow is also a power within us. It shoots an arrow, which is a strong intention. We cannot, at the same time, intend to live more life and more death.

[4]*In no way can a servant serve lords two:* A person cannot serve Spirit and an indoctrinating, false-god leader.

[5]*No man drinks wine old and desires to drink wine new:* No person listens to old dogma and immediately desires to listen to new wisdom from Spirit.

[6]*They do not pour wine new into wineskins old so that they not split open:* Spirit does not pour wisdom about how to live life fully into a person trapped by his attachment to things, money, friends, gurus, or past indoctrinated beliefs and traditions. Such a man could not embrace this wisdom without splitting himself in two with confusion.

Buddha (Ch. 6) also says that we cannot be on both ways at once:

The wise man leaves the dark Way for the light Way.[1]	[1]*The wise man leaves the dark Way for the Light Way:* The light seeker circumcises himself of the Mind Way for the Soul Way.
He leaves his securities to discover joy on the difficult Way.[2]	[2]*He leaves his securities to discover joy on the difficult Way:* He circumcises himself of his false securities to discover the joy in being one with Spirit on the Soul Way.

Summary

Throughout his journey to the Promised Earth, Abraham asked Spirit to guide him in all things, from what she was to say to his wife, to how he was to herd his sheep, to where they were to camp. Spirit also helped him understand how he could continually circumcise himself of his male's desire to lead him into the Dark Experience.

The Soul Way

The Mind Way

A person circumcises himself from his indoctrinators and their dogmas.

↑

A person physically circumcises himself to demonstrate his faithfulness to his indoctrinators and their dogmas.

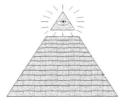

The Soul Way

The Mind Way

A person rides one horse, serves one lord, and pulls one bow.

↑

A person tries to ride two horses, to serve two lords, and to pull two bows.

A person lives a life of clarity and singleness.

↑

A person lives a life of confusion and compromises.

CHAPTER THIRTEEN

THE ABRAHAM ALLEGORY: SACRIFICE YOUR ISAAC

Abraham's wife, Sarah, birthed a son by the name of Isaac. He was Abraham's most cherished possession, *not* Spirit. With that one last attachment, Abraham was trying to serve two lords: Spirit and his ego voice, which told him to be remembered and honored through his progeny.

One day, Spirit demanded that Abraham live the Covenant fully by using his inner "sword" to sacrifice his attachment to Isaac, his most precious possession. To "sacrifice" means to de-identify from his son to be oneself. In Genesis 22:1-18, we read the dramatic allegory that tells us both how Abraham sacrificed Isaac and how we must do the same to live in the Promised Earth.

> *And the Gods tested Abraham. They said, "Take your son, your only son Isaac, whom you love, and go into the land of Moriah and offer him there as a burnt offering upon one of the mountains to which I will guide you..."*

> *So, Abraham took the wood for the burnt offering and laid it upon Isaac, his son. And he took the fire in his hand and a knife, and they went both of them together.*

> *And Isaac said to his father Abraham, "My father!" And he said, "Here am I, my son." He said, "Behold, the fire, and the wood, but where is the lamb for a burnt offering?" Abraham said, "The Gods will provide the lamb for a burnt offering, my son." So, they went both of them together (Gen. 22: 1-7).*

Jesus summarizes this chapter in a *Gospel of Thomas* poem (Saying 42):

> You come into being[1]
>
> As you pass away.[2]

[1] *You come into being:* You become one with your divine self

[2] *As you pass away:* As you sacrifice your false identities.

The Gods tested Abraham:

A "test" is a choice to live on the Soul Way or the Mind Way.

God tested Abraham and said to him, "Abraham!" And he answered, "Here am I."

Abraham answered, "Here am I." Abraham became present with himself and with Spirit in the present.

The Gods said, "Take your son, your only son Isaac, whom you love, and go to the land of Moriah, and offer him there as a burnt offering upon one of the mountains to which I shall guide you."

Only son: Metaphorically, it is one's most cherished false self and the dogma associated with it.

Exercise:

A Question for Reflection: Right now, you, the reader, ask yourself: "Can you say, "Here am I?" In other words, are you living in the "now," or in the past or future?"

My answer: If I notice that I am living in the past or future, I know that I am tempted to "eat" (enjoy) the Dark Experience: anxiety, worry, sadness, depression—alternating with superficial happiness and excitement. Those emotions only happen when I am not in the moment. If I can say, "Here am I," I am one with myself and Spirit, and I can now talk with my Guide about how to "go" more deeply into the Promised Earth.

Exercise:

A Question for Reflection: Right now, you, the reader, ask yourself: "Am I unconsciously promoting, defending, or worrying about something or someone I cherish, such as my money, my job, my family, or what people think of me?"

My answer: When I say, "Yes," I know that I have discovered my Isaac that I need to sacrifice to be totally committed to Spirit and to being in the Promised Earth. If I do not sacrifice (de-identify from) people and things, I will die a thousand deaths in a foreign land (Nod).

The Gods said, "Take your son, your only son Isaac, whom you love, and go to the land of Moriah, and offer him there as a burnt offering upon one of the mountains to which I shall guide you."

Offer him there as a burnt offering. An "offering" that is "burnt" is one given up in burning love. For example, when one gives up his identification with his appearance to identify with the life he shares with Spirit and with others, he can only do that in love. If he tries to do that in hate, he will see himself as "bad." That will send him even more deeply into the Dark Experience.

Upon one of the mountains there: To go upon a "mountain" means to go high in oneself to communicate intuitively (with one's third-eye and ear) with Spirit. Thus, one can go up on a mountain in a park or in a bedroom—any place that is comforting and quiet.

The symbols for going high on one's inner mountain to obtain intuitive insights are the ones that we have been using:

When one lives more fully from the top of the mountain, he wisely loves all; therefore, he becomes the mountain. So, a pyramid can symbolize two things: the need to use high-level intuitive insights to live in the Promised Earth, and a person who has become solidly, and wisely himself above the dark, dead, unwise world.

Throughout the world, ancient cultures erected pyramids. They understood, perhaps, that to develop oneself into a wise, noble person, one needed to use primarily his third-eye and ear. They buried their nobility in the pyramids as way of saying, most likely, that the person within lived as a strong, wise, dominating mountain.

> *When they came to the place of which the Gods had told him, Abraham built an altar there, and laid the wood in order, and bound Isaac, his son, and laid him on the altar, upon the wood (Gen 22:9).*

When he came to the place of which God had told him: When he became still, in the moment, ready to be with Spirit on his inner mountain.

Abraham built an altar there. Abraham opened his heart.

Abraham bound Isaac, his son, and laid him on the altar, upon the wood ('ets):

The Hebrew word "ʿets" means "wood" or "tree." Here it means both. The tree is the Tree of the Knowledge of Life. So, Abraham used that Tree to unconditionally wise-love Isaac.

> *Then Abraham put forth his hand and took the knife to slay his son. But the angel of Being called to him from heaven and said, "Abraham, Abraham!" And he said, "Here am I."*
>
> *He said, "Do not lay your hand on the boy or do anything to him; for now, I know that you fear Being seeing you have not withheld your son, your only son, from me" (Gen 22:2).*

Abraham took the knife to slay his son. The "knife" is the inner "sword" necessary to divide his false self from his real self. For example, a person who identifies with his appearance could use his "sword" to slay his Isaac by choosing to befriend people whom others consider "ugly."

Do not lay your hand on the boy or do anything to him. Do not harm the object of your attachment. For example, if one is attached to his appearance, one de-identifies from what people think of his looks without damaging his body. Or, in another example, if one has built a false self around money, one can sacrifice himself by simply not identifying with that false security. There is no need to divest oneself of it.

For now, I know that you fear Being. For now, I (Being) know that you correctly fear the consequences of not being your real self.

And Abraham lifted his eye and looked, and behold, behind him was a ram, caught in a thicket by his horns; and Abraham went and took the ram and offered it up as a burnt offering instead of his son.

So Abraham called the name of that place Jehovah-jireh (Gen 22:13-14).

Abraham lifted his eye and looked: Abraham understood the situation with his single-eye:

And behold, behind him was a ram, caught in a thicket by his horns: And with intuitive insight, Abraham saw his beautiful male side, trapped by its attachments. In other words, Abraham looked in the mirror and saw how he was in darkness, caught by his obsession with his son, and through him, with his legacy.

Abraham went and took the ram, and offered it up as a burnt offering instead of his son: Abraham took his male, ego desire to be important through his son, and in love, sacrificed it. In other words, he stopped identifying with his legacy. He saw it "over there," perfect-as-is. It was no longer him. He became free to be himself.

So, Abraham called the name of that place, "Jehovahjireh." Abraham called the name of that place within himself wherein he is one with Spirit, "Being will provide."

> *And the angel of Being called to Abraham a second time from heaven, and said…"Because you have done this and have not withheld your son, your only son, abundantly, I will bless you and multiply your descendants as the stars in the heavens and the grains of sand on the seashore. Further, your descendants will possess the gate of their enemies, and by your descendants, all the nations of the earth will be blessed because you have obeyed my voice" (Gen 22:15-18).*

The angel of Being called to Abraham a second time from heaven: Spirit talked to Abraham when he was living in his new-found higher level of truth and love.

Because you have done this, and have not withheld your son, your only son, abundantly I will bless you: Because you chose to be your own unique version of divine, wise love in the world, even if it means that no one will ever remember and honor you through your son, I will give you more life in the Promised Earth.

And I will multiply your descendants as the stars in the heavens and the grains of sand on the seashore. I will ensure that your legacy will be known and lived by your abundant followers on the Soul Way.

Your descendants will possess the gate of their enemies. Your followers will conquer those on the Mind Way.

By your descendants, all the nations of the land will be blessed: Your followers will be a light to all of those on the Mind Way.

Because you have obeyed My voice: Because you obeyed My guidance and not that of your snake.

SACRIFICE

Probably from the beginning of recorded time, people noted that when a group did certain things, it did or did not rain. They also saw that when an individual prayed for a sick person, the person sometimes became well. At other times, prayer seemed not to affect someone's health, nor did it bring needed rain. They concluded that an intelligent God was sometimes helping them and sometimes causing problems. So, the question many asked was: "How do I (or we) manipulate this intelligent being to do what we want him or her to do?"

A common answer for the ancients was that the intelligent god (or gods) wants something from them before he or she responds favorably to their needs. That notion probably arose from watching human interaction when someone responds positively because he or she has received a gift that the giver sacrificed money or time to obtain. That idea seems to have led to the practice of trying to please this intelligent God or Gods with some kind of sacrifice.

Today, many people try to manipulate an intelligent god or gods to get what they want through prayer, fasting, doing rituals, following a set of laws (such as the Torah Laws) believing dogma (such as is found in the Koran) avoiding things (such as walking under a ladder) or carrying things (such as a rabbit's foot or amulet). All of those things require some kind of personal sacrifice.

Others, today, don't recognize that things happen because of human activity. Instead, they see events happening by chance or "natural selection." That leads them to worry about having the things necessary to avoid bad things happening and to make good things occur.

Those on the Soul Way do not pray or do rituals to change what is going on. They know that Spirit works through every event to help those who desire the Light or Dark Experience get what they want and live the consequences.

Those on the Soul Way know that the only beneficial sacrifice is that of leaving false-god leaders and their garments. In that way, one receives what he most deeply seeks, a wonderful life in the Promised Earth.

Jesus' Notion of Sacrifice

Jesus summed up how we make the beneficial sacrifice in a few lines in *The Gospel of Thomas* (Saying 69a):

The blessed ones

They
are
those

Who
have persecuted themselves
in their own hearts.

To persecute oneself is to sacrifice one's false self to become independently real. Jesus also says that in the following Saying 68 in *The Gospel of Thomas*:

You
are
the bessed ones[1]

[1]*Blessed ones:* Those who live the Covenant.

When
they
hate you

And
persecute you[2]

[2]*When they hate you:* When they hate you for living a high level of truth and love. For example, when they despise you for abandoning their adored indoctrinator.

For
they
will discover
not any place[3]

[3]*Place:* A false self within a person that has not been confronted and removed.

Where
you
have
not persecuted
yourselves.[4]

[4]*For they will discover not any place where you have not persecuted yourselves:* For they will not find a weakness in your character that you have not examined and eliminated.

Exercise:

Questions for Reflection:

1. What is the thing or person you worry about most?

2. What is the event you regret the most?

3. What do you desire the most?

My answer: Unless my answer to those questions is something like: "To be more in the Promised Earth," I have identified my Isaac that I need to sacrifice to be more fulfilled in the Light experience.

For example, in the past, what I desired most was a soul-mate. I then realized that that person was my Isaac that I needed to sacrifice to be whole, fully alive, and worthy of such a great partner. So I stopped dating, and after five years, I was given her without seeking her.

The Distinction between "Circumcision" and "Sacrificing-Your-Isaac"

Circumcision is a metaphor for two actions:

1. The commitment to live the Covenant, and

2. The process of removing a garment, that is, a false self and its associated beliefs.

Sacrificing-Your-Isaac is a metaphor for removing your *most treasured* garment, that is, your *most guarded* false self and its associated beliefs.

Summary

THE SOUL WAY

THE MIND WAY

Identify and sacrifice your Isaacs.
↑
Cling to your false-god supporters and their false securities.

Be single, powerful, free, and real in the Light Experience.
↑
Remain duplicitous, weak, and imprisoned in the Dark Experience.

CHAPTER FOURTEEN

THE JACOB ALLEGORY

INTRODUCTION

Abraham died. His grandson, Jacob, also wanted to live the Covenant. Spirit obliged in a way that tested Jacob (Genesis 32: 24-28):

One night, Jacob was alone. A man appeared and struggled with Jacob until the breaking of the day.

Then, the man said, "Let me go, for the day breaks." But Jacob replied, "I will not let you go unless you bless me."

Then, the man said, "Let me go, for the day breaks."

But Jacob replied, "I will not let you go unless you bless me."

The man asked him, "What is your name?"

He answered, "Jacob."

Then, the man said, "Your name will no longer be Jacob, but Israel, because you have the power of the Gods and have overcome your humanity."

One night: A "night" is a Dark Experience. One can be in it for minutes or years.

One night, Jacob was alone: In a Dark Experience, Jacob found himself separated from Spirit, from his real self, and from All.

A man appeared and struggled with Jacob. Spirit's angel provided Jacob with a choice to "go" to the Light Experience or to "go" to the

Dark Experience. He painfully "struggled" to figuratively sacrifice his Isaac, his most treasured attachment on the Mind Way.

Remember, in the Garden Allegory, Eve told us that when anyone, like Jacob, decides to use his female side to birth a new, higher, more fulfilled self, he and she would struggle in much pain: (Gen 3:16):

To the woman Being-Gods said:

[1]*Spirit said, "I will multiply your sorrow greatly in pregnancy:* Spirit said, "You will be sorrowful when you realize you are in the Dark Experience and long to be in the light Experience."

"I will multiply greatly your sorrow in pregnancy,[1]

In pain you shall bring forth children[2]

[2]*In pain, you will bring forth children:* Each time you circumcise yourself from your Isaac to birth your real self, you will be in psychological pain.

And your desire will be for the man to rule you."[3]

[3]*And your desire will be for the man to rule you:* And your pain will arise because one part of you wants your male side to keep you in the Dark Experience.

Jacob's woman wants to "bring" him "forth" to a higher level of life. His man wants to "guard" his most treasured false identity. So, he painfully struggles to let "go" of his old, comfortable, enjoyable self to "go" with Spirit's guidance to a new, more enjoyable Promised Earth.

The man struggled with Jacob until the breaking of the day. The angel struggled with Jacob until he began to leave the Dark Experience and move into the Light Experience.

Then, the man said, "Let me go, for the day breaks." Then, the man said, "You are somewhat in the light, so stop struggling."

But Jacob replied, "I will not let you go unless you bless me." Jacob replied, "I will not let you go until you give me the full Light Experience. In other words, "I am not satisfied until I have sacrificed myself *totally*. Then I will be the perfect, beautiful ram offering to Spirit, to myself, and to All."

The man asked him, "What is your name?" Spirit asked him, "What is your current most treasured identity that you need to give up to live fully in the Promised Earth?"

He answered, "Jacob." He answered, "Jacob" (which means Supplanter). (Earlier, Jacob, with the help of his mother, Rebecca, tricked his father into supplanting his older brother with him as the family birthright. In that way, Jacob identifies himself with carrying on the family spirit/genetic line of Abraham).

Then, the man said, "Your name will no longer be Jacob, but "Israel:"

Israel: One who, with the guidance of Spirit, struggles to leave the Mind Way for the Soul Way.

Then, the man said, "Your name will no longer be Jacob, but Israel, because you have the power of the Gods and have overcome your humanity." Then, Spirit said, "Your identity will no longer be with your family in your role as "supplanter." Instead, you will now be called "Israel" because you became what you are, powerful, divine life, not what they wanted you to be.

ISRAELITES

After Jacob received his new name, each of those who follow him possesses a new name: "Israelite" (A person who, with the guidance of Spirit, continually struggles not only to circumcise himself of his small, dark, false selves but also to sacrifice his most treasured Isaac (huge false self).

An Israelite, then, is a person who does not identify with his family, traditions, dogmas, or anything else, except Spirit guidance. He lives the Covenant to "go" from the land of his tribes and family to "go" to the Promised Earth.

EXERCISE:

A QUESTION FOR REFLECTION: Pretend that like Jacob, you must struggle between two very important options that figuratively boil down to going *east* or *west*.

To decide, you go to your favorite, beautiful place where you can communicate in stillness with Spirit. There, you suspend all of your past beliefs and become open to being inspired. After some time, you sense strongly, "To be your true self, you need to go *east*. There you will have a more fulfilled life and be of the greatest wise-love benefit to humanity."

Then, you leave your beautiful place and go to your family and ask for their advice about whether to go **east** or **west**. They tell you that if you go **east**, you will betray the family values and traditions. As a result, they will be embarrassed in the community. Further, your spouse tells you that you can expect a divorce should you go **east**.

So, because you wonder if they are right, you go to your boss at work who seems to possess sound judgment. She listens to you and then tells you that unless you go *west*, she will fire you.

Confused, you ask leading clergy and theologians in many religions, who, in turn, consult their scriptures and the opinions of past commentators. They tell you that unless you go **west**, you will be a grave sinner.

Exasperated, you consult with leading philosophers and psychologists. After they read the relevant research and the writings of others going back thousands of years, they tell you that dire consequences will happen to you and others if you go *east*.

Because you continue to feel confused, you go back to your peaceful place, become very still, and invite Paul, the Apostle, to appear to you. In a short time, he does. You then explain your problem and seek his advice. He tells you that if you go **east**, you will demonstrate that you do not believe in Jesus' redemption of humankind on the cross, in his resurrection, and in his coming again for the final judgment. Thus, if you go **east**, you will not be saved.

And so you go to Spirit again. Again Spirit shows you clearly that you should go **east**.

In more confusion, you become still and invite John the Evangelist to talk to you. Sure enough, he quickly appears. After you explain the situation, he tells you that if you go **east**, you will demonstrate that you do not believe in the person of Jesus; thus, you will go to hell.

Frustrated, you decide to consult the Old Testament. Yes, indeed, the Torah tells you that in your circumstance, you should go **west**.

"Then," you think, "Maybe my solution is not in the Bible." So, you ask Mohammed to appear to you. He does. You explain your problem, and he says, "Look, if you read the Koran, you will notice that I clearly say that you will be a non-believer and attack Allah if you go **east**."

Exasperated, you ask Eve, Abraham, Buddha, and Jesus to appear to you. They come to you as one group. You again explain to them your situation. They listen, and then, they smile and disappear.

Now, something does not feel right. So in painful confusion, you go back up on your beautiful mountain and communicate again with Spirit. After a half-hour, you are shown in a compelling vision why you need to go *east* to be yourself as a unique gift to the world. It is clear to you that only by going *east* can you unconditionally wise-love All.

DECISION TIME: If you, the reader, got all of this advice, would you go **east** or **west**?

MY ANSWER: If I go *east*, I will be an Israelite who is guided by Spirit to the Promised Earth (the Garden of Eden). If you go west, I will be a "Dogmaite" (my term), that is, a person who is guided by dogmas, usually those from the mouths of others.

THE SOUL WAY

THE MIND WAY

Lived by people who are
Israelites

↑

Lived by people who are
Dogmaites

CHAPTER FIFTEEN

THE JOSEPH ALLEGORY

JOSEPH

Jacob (Israel) had twelve sons. Only one, his favorite, was an Israelite. His name was Joseph.

Joseph's eleven Dogmaite brothers were jealous of his relationship with their father. To get rid of their adversary, the brothers sold Joseph to traders. They, in turn, sold him into slavery in Egypt.

To hide what they did, the guilty brothers painted goat's blood on Joseph's coat and showed it to Israel. Believing that his son was dead, Israel went into deep morning.

JESUS AND DIVISION

In *The Gospel of Thomas*, Saying 16, Jesus wrote about the division that happens between people when some are Israelites (like Joseph and Israel), and others are Dogmaites (like the eleven brothers):

For
there
are
five

Who
will come to be
in a house.

[1] *There are three who will come against two:* Those living the Mind Way in a house or any community will "come against" those living on the Soul Way.

There
are
three

Who
will come to be
against two[1]

And
two
will come to be
against three

The father
against the son

And
the son
against the father

And
they
will stand on their feet[2]

[2] *They will stand on their feet:* They will be strong and powerful because they stand on their Soul Way principles.

[3] *They being single ones:* They being united and not divided within themselves. They who do not "ride two horses," "pull two bows," or "serve two masters."

They
being
single ones.[3]

JOSEPH IN EGYPT

In Egypt, Joseph became the wise advisor to the Pharaoh. In that position, he was able to bring Israel and his eleven sons and household to live with him.

At first, Israel and his sons did not recognize Joseph. When they finally did, and when they saw that Joseph forgave them, they became Israelites and lived with him. After many years, the descendants of the twelve sons became the twelve tribes, all of them enslaved to the Dogmaite, Egyptian Pharaoh.

JESUS AND DOGMAITE PHAROAHS

Metaphorically, Egypt is the world today. The world's pharaohs brainwash people with their dogmas about theology, economics, politics, and social traditions and customs. When people embrace these dogmas, they may become enslaved to a leader and his organization, which can be a dark, controlling cult hiding behind words and actions denoting love of others. Jesus warns us of this in *The Gospel of Thomas* (Saying 3):

If
they
should say to you
this:[1]

[1]*If they should say to you this:* If religious, political, parental, educational, or other dark, "world" pharaohs should indoctrinate you…

"Behold!"[2]

[2]*Behold:* Be in awe of my dogmas that you need to know.

The Kingdom
is in (my) heaven"[3]

[3]*The Kingdom is in (my) heaven:* Your fulfilled way to be is in my level and way of thinking.

Then
the birds[4]

[4]*Birds:* Ideas, especially beliefs.

of their heaven
will come to be
first
before you.[5,6]

[5]*Then the birds of their heaven will come to be before you:* This phrase refers to Exodus 20:3—the first commandment. It tells us: "Do not put false gods (pharaohs) before you."

[6]*Then the birds of their heaven come to be first before you:* Then, the indoctrinating pharaohs and their dogmas will be your false gods.

If

they

should say to you

this:

Behold!

The Kingdom

is

in (my) sea"[7,8]

Then

the fish[9]

will come to be

first

before you.[10]

[7]*The sea:* A "sea" is our emotions. We are sometimes, for example, awash in our emotions.

[8]*The Kingdom is in (my) sea:* Your fulfilled way to be will be found in my emotionally conveyed dogmas.

[9]*Fish:* Felt ideas and beliefs.

[10]*Then the fish will come to be first before you:* Then the indoctrinators' emotional, often illogical ideas will become your false gods.

In this poem, Jesus describes two kinds of indoctrinating pharaohs: those who convince primarily with logic and those who teach primarily with emotion. The former preach logical, abstract dogmas (birds); the latter manipulate people into following their way of thinking and acting through emotionally-based, often illogical dogmas.

The dark "world" teaches us that our safety and fulfillment happens when we embrace correct dogmas about God, family, friends, country, money, etc. As a result, people take vows, pledges, and oaths to theologies, philosophies, people, flags, things, and the organizations that promote them. Once they do that, they enslave themselves in an Egypt (organization) under the control of a grand pharaoh and his priests. There, they become dead, dark Dogmaites.

Israelites do not do live by steadfast faith in dogmas.

- They continually give up lower level beliefs to envision at a higher level of truth and wise-love.

- They listen to others but make their own decisions.

- They are the disrupters of the world of the Dogmaites.

- They cannot be trusted to be the same every day.

- They live to evolve, not to conform.

- Generally, they do not believe anything that they do not first experience.

Thus, an Israelite would never believe in a God that he does not experience. Nor would he believe that God was one or many unless he experienced that. And then, he would be open to experiencing God differently in the next moment.

When an Israelite asks a personal question like what will happen after he physically dies, he goes apart, becomes one with Spirit, and "reveals" his answer. He may see the answer in a vision, in the laughter of a child, in a verbal assault by an enemy, or the lyrics of a song. He lets Spirit use any medium to show him what he wants to know. He grounds himself in reality, not in blind beliefs, which are often superstitions.

An Israelites may ask a pharaoh or anyone else for their answers, however, he will always return to Spirit guidance to make his own decisions.

SUMMARY:

There are only two kinds of people in the universe:

DOGMAITES	ISRAELITES
Lives from his own or another's dogmas.	Lives from his own experience.
Indoctrinates others with their own or official answers:	Empowers others to discover their answers:
Steadfastly lives former beliefs.	Continually suspends former beliefs, re-experiences himself, others, and the world, and then creates new tentative beliefs.
Finds security in his beliefs.	Finds his security in the *process* of personally evolving in wise-love.
Dreams of a time when all conflicts end because everyone lives his dogmas exactly the way he does.	Dreams of a time when all conflicts end because everyone empowers everyone else to be true to themselves.
Lives in the past and future	Lives in the present
To promote and defend his dogma-based ego, he ignores, distorts, and invents facts; and avoids and attacks personal criticism.	With no ego to promote and defend, he welcomes facts and personal criticism that show him his errors.

CHAPTER SIXTEEN

THE MOSES ALLEGORY: I AM WHO I AM.

The twelve tribes remained enslaved in Egypt for over 200 years. Finally, Spirit chose a man by the name of "Moses" to lead them out of Egypt (Exodus 3:4-15):

The Gods said to Moses, "I am the Gods of your father, the Gods of Abraham, the Gods of Isaac, and the Gods of Jacob…I, Being, have seen the affliction of my people who are in Egypt and have heard their cry because of their taskmasters. I know their sufferings; so, I have come to rescue them from the hand of the Egyptians and to bring them up out of that land into a good and broad earth, an earth flowing with milk and honey… Come, I will send you to Pharaoh that you may bring forth my people, the sons of Israel, out of Egypt."

But Moses said to the Gods, "If I come to the sons of Israel and say to them, 'The Gods of your ancestors has sent me to you,' and they ask me, 'What is Gods' name?' what shall I say to them?" The Gods said to Moses, "I am who I am."

I am the Gods of your father, the Gods of Abraham, the Gods of Isaac, and the Gods of Jacob…I have seen the affliction of my people who are in Egypt and have heard their cry because of their taskmasters; I know their sufferings.

We are reading an allegory that may be based on some historical facts. As such, the narrative describes us today. Our world is Egypt, where most people are on the Mind Way. Our churches, political parties, and other indoctrinating organizations are our Egypts. Our "taskmasters" can be clergy, politicians, professors, commentators, parents, and ourselves. These pharaohs indoctrinate people with personal answers rather than empower them to use Spirit to discover insights on their own.

I know their sufferings. We suffer when we are divided—between our real and false selves, between our real selves and Spirit, and between our real selves and the real selves of others. When people call others who differ in race, theology, income, appearance, etc. "bad," they cause conflicts that result externally in discrimination, persecution, and murder, and internally in emotional health problems. To be one with ourselves and others, which is the only way to solve our problems, we need to eat of the Tree of the Knowledge of Life, live the Covenant, circumcise ourselves, and sacrifice our Isaacs.

I have come to rescue them from the hand of the Egyptians: The word "hand" signifies "control." As an allegory, the Moses saga teaches us how to "go" from the "hand" of any Egypt or pharaoh to become our real selves.

I have come to bring them into good and broad earth, earth flowing with milk and honey...I have come to bring you into the Promised Earth (the Light Experience).

Milk symbolizes protein, and honey, carbohydrates. Together they are metaphors for the inspired wisdom needed in the Promised Earth. Milk is the kind of inspired insights that are difficult to digest. Honey is the opposite—wisdom that we accept and integrate easily into our lives.

The Gods said: "Come, I will send you to Pharaoh that you may bring forth my people, the sons of Israel, out of Egypt." Spirit said, "Come, I will send you to a pharaoh to ask permission to lead his followers out of his Egypt onto the Soul Way."

But Moses said to the Gods, "If I come to the Israelites and say to them, 'The Gods of your ancestors have sent me to you,' and they ask me, 'What is (Gods') names?' what shall I say to them?" The Gods said to Moses, "I am who I am."

The Israelites possessed the stories about Abraham and his Israelite descendants. They knew that their God's "name" (essence) was "I am who I am." In other words, God is himself, and he wants all people to be their unique divine selves. They are that to the degree that they can say, "I am who I am."

Buddha's Goal

Buddha (Ch. 6) also tells us that our goal is to be who we are.

The wise man
becomes himself
a light
pure
and
shining free.

So
master yourself
by living from your heart
and
by seeking the highest consciousness.

Exercise:

A Question for Reflection: Can you say, "I am who I am" if you also unconsciously say:

1. I am my job.

2. I am my reputation.

3. I am my family.

4. I am my sexual orientation.

5. I am my religious faith.

6. I am my political party.

7. I am my nation.

8. I am my sports team.

9. I am my money.

10. I am my things.

MY ANSWER: No. When I identify with anyone or anything other than my core self, I am not saying, "I am who I am." I am saying, "I am my false self or selves."

EXERCISE:

A Situation: Let us suppose that you, the reader, went to your beautiful, quiet place where you listen to Spirit. There, you were told to go to the neighborhood Church (or Mosque, or Temple) and meet with the organization's Pharaoh. After introducing yourself, you are to explain to him that he suppresses his congregation by indoctrinating them with dogma. Then, you are to explain how you would like permission to lead his members to the Promised Earth on the Soul Way. There, they would find the fulfillment, freedom, and inner and outer unity that they deeply desire.

A QUESTION FOR REFLECTION: Would you follow Spirit's guidance?

MY ANSWER: If I did do it, I would expect rejection from the Church, Mosque, or Temple pharaoh (as is about to happen to Moses).

Exercise:

Questions for Reflection:

1. Why was Jesus murdered?

2. Would Jesus be murdered today?

My answers:

1. Why was Jesus murdered? **My answer:** He was teaching people to "go" from the control of religious and secular pharaohs and their organizations to "go" into the Promised Earth by following Spirit's guidance. Thus, Jewish and Roman secular and religious leaders killed him because he was upsetting their Dogmaite establishments.

2. Would he suffer the same fate today? **My answer:** Yes, if he did not possess a security guard. Religious and secular extremists would murder him in the name of Spirit or the right order.

Summary

Israelites are persecuted today by pharaohs. That happens both because they do not support any Dogmaite organization that teaches people to identify with dogmas, rituals, titles, roles, rules, buildings, flags, constitutions, vows, and indoctrinating leaders; and because they lead people out of the Mind Way onto the Soul Way.

CHAPTER SEVENTEEN

THE MOSES ALLEGORY: CHOOSE YOUR GOD

After a period of indecisiveness, Moses and his brother, Aaron, initiate the first of many requests to the Pharaoh to let the Israelites "go" from the Dogmaite land, Egypt. We read about Pharaoh's reaction in Exodus:

> *Pharaoh responded: "Who is Being that I should obey that One's voice and let Israel go? I do not know Being, nor will I let the sons of Israel go." (Exodus 5:2)*

> *Moses returned to Being and said, "After I went to Pharaoh to speak in your name, he has brought trouble to the people. You have not delivered your people at all."*

> *Then Being said to Moses, "Now you will see what I will do to Pharaoh. I will compel him to let them go (Exodus 5:2-6:1)*

Pharaoh responded: "Who is Being that I should obey that One's voice and let Israel 'go?'" Pharaoh replied: "What is the nature and power of Spirit that compels me to make His voice more important than that of our God?"

Pharaoh responded: "I do not know Being."

There are two kinds of gods. The Dogmaites know One with the Tree of the Knowledge of Good and Bad. It is a God that demands that people worship him by observing rituals, by obeying laws and clergy, by believing blind beliefs, and by sacrificing things other than themselves to be good and to get good things. That is the God of the Pharaoh.

The Israelites know Spirit with the Tree of the Knowledge of Life. This God asks for nothing except that people be the divine, perfect-as-is selves that they are. To do that, they need to leave the indoctrinating voices of theologians, clergy, and other authorities to have give-and-take communication with Spirit. For example, notice how Moses talks to Being:

Moses returned to Being and said, "Since I went to Pharaoh to speak in your name, he has brought trouble to the people. You have not delivered your people at all."

Then Being said to Moses, "Now you will see what I will do to Pharaoh. I will compel him to let them go.

In this passage, Moses and Being communicate back and forth with each other as two people who are close, intimate friends. This Israelite Spirit does not seek to be worshiped as someone totally other, but rather as one who shares the same core life.

JESUS' INTIMATE RELATIONSHIP WITH SPIRIT

Jesus considers Spirit more than a friend. He calls Spirit his intimate spouse in *The Gospel of Thomas* (Saying 75):

There
are
many
standing there
at the door;[1]

[1] *There are many standing there at the door:* There are many Dogmaites standing around outside the ultimate intimate experience.

Rather
the single ones[2]
are
those

[2] *Single Ones:* Israelites who are one with their real selves.

Who
will go into the place
of marriage.[3]

[3] *The single ones are those who will go into the place of marriage:* The Israelites are those who leave their minds and become one with their soul where they can communicate intimately with Spirit.

Exercise:

Questions for Reflection:

1. Do you think that another person can fulfill your deepest intimacy needs?

2. Do you think that our desire for deep intimacy permeates the world's romantic songs and elaborate marriage ceremonies?

3. Do you think that by possessing an intimate marriage with Spirit that you will more likely have deep intimacy with other people?

My answers:

1. Do you think that another person can fulfill your deepest intimacy needs? **My answer:** No. When I expect that another completely meet my intimacy desires, I am always disappointed. Further, I later realize that I was not unconditionally loving the person but instead loving on the condition that the person fulfills my needs. That kind of love results ultimately in more distance between me and another.

2. Do you think that our desire for deep, complete intimacy permeates the world's romantic songs and elaborate marriage ceremonies? **My answer:** Yes. We seem to soul-know that we are not alone and that someone loves us unconditionally. So, instead of going up on our mountain and empowering our third eye and ear to teach us how to possess intimacy with Spirit, we project our needs on another human who will never fulfill them.

3. Do you think that by possessing an intimate marriage with Spirit that you will more likely have deep intimacy with other people? **My answer:** When I am united intimately with Spirit, I find the security and insights to unconditionally wise-love myself and others.

Summary

We get the God that we choose.

Dogmaite God	Israelite God (Spirit)
People know this God with the Tree of the Knowledge of Good and Bad	People know this God (Spirit) with the Tree of the Knowledge of Life
If people want to be intimate with this God, they must perform rituals, obey laws, and blindly believe dogmas.	If people want to be intimate with this God (Spirit), they must live the Garden Command and the Covenant.
This God loves good people and punishes bad ones	This God (Spirit) wise-loves everyone and everything unconditionally.
This God has been called the "Old Testament God." He is also the God of the Koran and some of the New Testament.	This is the God (Spirit) of parts of the Old and New Testament.
This God authorizes theologians and clergy to teach and discipline people.	This God (Spirit) inspires people directly; consequently, there is no need for theologians or clergy.
People worship this God as "totally other."	People do not worship this God; rather, they have intimate conversations with Spirit as one does with a close friend.

CHAPTER EIGHTEEN

THE MOSES ALLEGORY: DIVIDE YOUR SEA

After a period of indecisiveness, Moses and his brother, Aaron, went to the Pharaoh to seek permission to lead the Israelites out of Egypt. We learn in Exodus 5:22-6:1 what happened.

> *Moses returned to Being and said, "Since I went to Pharaoh to speak in your name, he has brought trouble on the people, and you have not delivered your people at all."*

> *Then Being said to Moses, "Now, you will see what I will do to Pharaoh. I will compel him to let them go.*

Being said: "Now, you will see what I will do to Pharaoh. I will compel him to let them go."

After each of Pharaoh's refusals to let the Israelites "go" from his dogma control, we read about successive calamities that Spirit inflicted on the Egyptians— from drought, starvation, and plagues to the impotence of the Pharaoh's priests to do anything to stop the tragedies (Exodus: 6-12). In this way, Abraham, through this Allegory, tells us that we (personally and as a global people) will suffer when we do not live on the Soul Way.

Finally, Pharaoh agrees to let the Israelites "go" because he believes that Spirit caused the problems afflicting his people (Exodus 12:31):

> *And the Pharaoh summoned Moses and Aaron by night, and said, "Rise, **go forth** from among my people, both you and the people of Israel; and go and serve Being.*

In this short paragraph, the Pharaoh told Moses and Aaron to live Abraham's Covenant. They are to "go forth from among "my people" (the Egyptian Dogmaites) to be led by Spirit to "go" to the Promised Earth.

MOSES DIVIDES THE SEA

Moses obeys Pharaoh and marches before the Israelites to the sea. When they observe that the water blocks them, Moses solves the problem (Exodus 14: 21):

> *Then, after Moses stretched out his hand over the sea, Being drove the sea back by a strong east wind all night and made the dry earth. As a result, the waters were divided. Then Moses led Israel onward.*

Sea: Our emotions, especially our emotional attachments to our false selves and their associated beliefs.

Moses stretched out his hand over the sea: Moses conquered his emotions, not by denying them, but by properly using them to become still in the moment full of wise-love.

Being drove the sea back by a strong east wind.

Wind: Inspiration. Recall in Genesis 3:24 Eve told us that we enter the Garden of Eden (the Light Experience) in the east where the sun (light inspiration) rises:

So
Being-Gods
drove out the person

And
placed at the east
of the Garden
of Eden
a Cherubim
and
a flaming sword

*Which
turned around
to guard the Way
to the Tree of Life.*

Being drove the sea back by a strong east wind all night and made the dry earth. As a result, the waters were divided. Being provided the inspiration that Moses needed to conquer his dark (night) emotional attachments to his false selves. As a result, his unreceptive "land" became "dry earth" (receptive of seeds of inspiration), and his distracting emotions became "divided" from him.

Then Moses led Israel onward: Then Moses was able to lead the Israelites out of Pharaoh's control "onward" towards the Promised Earth (the Light Experience).

The Metaphorical Meaning of "Dividing the Sea."

Those who regard the exodus of the Israelites from Egypt as pure history have sought to prove how Moses could have divided the sea. However, the story is an allegory. We learn in the following poems by Buddha and Jesus that the "sea" is our sea of emotional attachments from which we all must be divided to be guided by Spirit.

Buddha (Ch. 24) said:

Thirty-six streams
attack you
in pleasurable lust.[1]

[1]*Thirty-six streams attack you in pleasurable lust:* You are full of wild emotions, going from sadness to excitement to...all because you are attached to your false selves.

O' slave of desire
float upon the streams.[2]

[2]*O' slave of desire, float upon the stream:* O' Dogmaite, do not run from your feelings; instead, observe them detachedly.

Seeker!
empty the boat
lighten the load
of desires and passions.[3]

[3]*Empty the boat of desire...* Empty your self of your identification with dogmas about what you need to be good and saved.

Go beyond this Way[4]
to the other shore[5]
where
the world dissolves[6]
and
everything
becomes clear.[7]

[4]*Go beyond this Way:* Go from the Mind Way.

[5]*To the other shore:* To the Soul Way.

[6]*Where the world dissolves:* Where you are free from the control of Dogmaites.

[7]*And everything becomes clear:* And you see things as they are rather than through the lens of dogma interpretation.

In Buddha's poem, to "float upon the streams" is another metaphor for Moses' act of "dividing the sea."

In another example, Mark in Chapter 4:35-41 of his Gospel presents Jesus as conquering his sea of emotions:

Jesus
said to them
on that day
evening having come to be:[1]

[1]*Evening having come to be:* Jesus and his disciples find themselves entering the Dark Experience.

"Let us
go into the other side."[2]

[2]*Let us go into the other side:* Let us "go" from this Dark Experience to "go" to the Light Experience on the "other side." (Notice that Mark uses Buddha's terminology: "the other side."

And
having let go the crowd,[3]
they
took him

[3]*Having let go of the crowd:* Having let "go" of the world's pharaohs and their Dogmaite followers.

As
he
was[4]
in the boat…

[4]*They took him as he was in the boat:* The disciples unconditionally wise-loved Jesus in their community (boat).

And
occurred
a great hurricane
of wind[5]

[5]*And occurred a great hurricane of wind:* As soon as they decided to leave the world's Pharaohs and their conformist followers, the disciples were inspired with ideas (the wind) that they interpreted as "bad."

And
the waves
were throwing themselves
into the boat[6]

So that already
the boat
was getting filled.[7]

And
he
was in the stern
upon the pillow
sleeping.[8]

So
they
woke him up[9]

And
chattered to him,[10]

"Teacher
not
it
is of concern
to you

That
we
are perishing?[11]

And
having raised up[12]
he
rebuked the wind[13]

[6]*The waves were throwing themselves into the boat:* Their emotions were threatening their community's peace.

[7]*The boat was getting filled:* Their community was getting filled with emotional upset.

[8]*Jesus was upon the pillow sleeping:* Jesus was one with Spirit, and therefore, unaffected by their upsetting ideas and emotions.

[9]*So they woke him up:* So, they asked him to help them with their ideas and emotions.

[10]*And they chattered to him:* And they fearfully shouted all kinds of things.

[11]*We are perishing:* The disciples believe their emotions that tell them that things are so bad that they could die (When we leave a lower level of truth and love, we feel like we are dying).

[12]*And having raised up:* And Jesus faced the emotional situation.

[13]*He rebuked the wind:* And he dismissed their ideas that told them that they were about to die."

And
said to the sea,

"Be silent!

Be muzzled!"[14]

[14]*And said to the sea, "Be silent, be muzzled:"* Jesus quieted their emotions.

And
the wind
abated,[15]

[15]*And the wind abated:* And their lives became manageable.

And
there
came to be a great calm.[16]

[16]*And there came to be a great calm:* And Jesus and the disciples became still in the moment.

And
he
said to them:

"Why
are you
cowardly?[17]

[17]*Why are you cowardly:* Why are you afraid to face your emotions?

Not yet
are
you
having faith?[18]

[18]*Not yet, are you having faith?* Do you not have faith that Spirit will guide you to conquer your emotions?

And
they feared
with a great fear[19]

[19]*And they feared a great fear:* And their fear of Jesus' power over his emotions added to their fear of their emotions.

And
they
chattered to one another:

"Who really
is this

That also
the wind
and the sea
obey him?"[20]

[20]*Who really is this that the wind and the sea obey him:* Who really is this man who can depend totally on Spirit to overcome emotional attachments?

This short allegory is one of seven composed by Mark in his Gospel to describe the process of facing and conquering one's emotional sea (Mk 3:9, 4:1, 4:35-41, 5:18-21, 6:32, 6:45-52, 8:10-13). Because the number "seven" means "perfect," and because we find Buddha's terms such as "other side," "boat," and "fear," Mark shouts to his audience who knew Buddha's sayings, "See, Jesus fulfilled Buddha's formula for personal development perfectly." Or, "See, Jesus can do what Buddha can do." Or, "Jesus is greater than Buddha."

SUMMARY

One must confront and rise above his sea of dark emotions to be guided by Spirit to the "other side" (the Promised Earth). Throughout the Bible, allegories describe people who do that. For example, in Genesis (6:13-9:29) we read about how Noah built a boat to float above his "flood" of emotions.

CHAPTER NINETEEN

THE MOSES ALLEGORY: KNOW INSPIRATION WITH THE TREE OF LIFE

After crossing the Sea, Moses led his people not into the Promised Earth, but rather, into the wilderness. A "wilderness" is a place devoid of much "water" (inspiration). We all enter the "wilderness" when we "go" from the control of our pharaohs because we have not yet learned to communicate continually with Spirit.

THE WILDERNESS OF MARAH

We learn what happened next to Moses and his followers in Exodus 15:22-26:

They went for three days in the wilderness and found no water. And when they came to Marah, they could not drink of the waters of Marah because it was bitter. And the people murmured against Moses, saying, "What shall we drink?"

Moses cried out to Being. Being showed him a tree to throw into the water. Having thrown it, the water was made sweet...

And Being said, "If you will listen and listen to the voice of Being-Gods, and do what is right in that One's sight and give ear to the commandments and keep the laws, I will not put the diseases upon you which I put upon the Egyptians, for I am Being that heals."

They went for three days. The number "three" symbolizes "a short period of transition."

They went three days in the wilderness and found no water. They went a short time without being guided by Spirit.

Eve, Abraham, and Jesus' messages imply that, in reality, there is no wilderness. Every thought and emotion inside us, and everything said and done outside of us is Spirit's guidance. When one "wakes up," one gradually realizes that nothing "just happens."

For example, Jesus said, "Seek, and you will find" (Matt. 7:7). That law describes perfect order, not chaos.

And when they came to Marah, they could not drink its waters because it was bitter.

When inspiration is "bitter," it results in emotional death. That happens when we know inspiration with the Tree of the Knowledge of Good and Bad. Historically, this "bitter" inspiration has marked significant events in human affairs.

For example, Hitler chose to know Jews and others with the Tree of the Knowledge of Good and Bad. When he did that, he viewed himself as good and his enemies as bad. He then used his inspiration to harm those that threatened him. As a result, he became more "bitter," that is, more unfulfilled in the Dark Experience.

Hitler could have chosen to know others with the Tree of the Knowledge of Life. If he did that, he would have been inspired to wise-love others. That would have resulted because he was drinking sweet water—light inspiration.

The people murmured against Moses, saying, 'What shall we drink? The people were "bitter" because they knew things as "bad" with the Tree of the Knowledge of Good and Bad. They wanted the Light experience, and they blamed Moses for not giving it to them.

Moses cried out to Being, and Being showed him a tree to throw into the water. After Moses cried out for guidance, Being reminded him that they needed to know inspired ideas with the Tree of the Knowledge of Life.

Having thrown it into the water, it was made sweet. After Moses knew inspiration with the Tree of the Knowledge of Life, he obtained the insights to become more alive.

And Being said, "If you will diligently listen to the voice of Being-Gods, and do what is right in that One's sight and will give ear to the commandments and keep the laws, I will put none of the diseases upon you which I put upon the Egyptians, for I am Being that heals." Spirit tells us continually, "If you live the Garden Command, you will not become emotionally sick."

Exercise:

A Question for Reflection: What mistake did Moses make after Spirit told him to throw the tree into the water to make it sweet?

My answer: Moses did not teach each of the Israelites to know their inspired ideas with the Tree of the Knowledge of Life. Instead, he became a pharaoh and indoctrinated them with his insights. In that way, the people became more dependent on him.

Summary

The Soul Way

The Mind Way

Israelites who know their inspired ideas primarily with the Tree of the Knowledge of Life.

Dogmaites who know their inspired ideas primarily with the Tree of the Knowledge of Good And Bad.

CHAPTER TWENTY

THE MOSES ALLEGORY: CONTINUALLY EAT INSPIRATION

THE WILDERNESS OF SIN

As they traveled, the people continued to be unwilling to communicate directly with Spirit (Exodus 16):

And the assembly of the sons of Israel came to the Wilderness of Sin and grumbled against Moses and Aaron. They said, "If only we had died by the hand of Being in the land of Egypt, when we sat by the pots of meat and when we ate our fill of bread. You have brought us out into this wilderness to kill this whole assembly with hunger."

Being said to Moses, "I have heard the complaining of the sons of Israel. Say to them, 'At twilight, you shall eat meat, and in the morning, you shall be filled with bread, and you shall know that I am Being-Gods.'"

It happened in the evening that quails came up and covered the camp, and in the morning, there was a layer of dew around the camp. When the layer of dew evaporated, behold on the surface of the wilderness was a fine, flaky substance as frost on the earth. And the house of Israel called its name, manna.

When the sons of Israel saw it, they said to one another, "What is it?" Moses said to them, "It is the bread that Being has given you to eat. Every person gathered what he needed to eat."

And Moses said to them, "Let no one leave any of it until morning."

But they did not listen to Moses; some left part of it until morning, and it bred worms and became foul. And Moses was angry with them.

Morning by morning they gathered it, each as much as he could eat; but when the sun grew hot, it melted.

And the assembly of the sons of Israel came to the Wilderness of Sin and grumbled against Moses and Aaron: When the Israelites were without inspiration, they became angry at Moses and his brother, Aaron, because they would not indoctrinate them with dogmas about how to live.

And the assembly grumbled against Moses and Aaron: "If only we had died by the hand of Being in the land of Egypt when we sat by the pots of meat and when we ate our fill of bread. You have brought us out into this wilderness to kill this whole assembly with hunger."

This passage revolves around the words "meat" (protein) and "bread" (carbohydrate), which are the two complementary kinds of food that people need in their diets. So metaphorically, "meat" and "bread" are the two kinds of inspired ideas we need for a fulfilled life. "Meat" is the kind of inspired insights that are difficult to digest. "Bread" is the opposite—wisdom that we accept and integrate easily into our lives.

Milk Symbolizes Complete Inspiration

Milk is both a protein and a carbohydrate. Jesus used the word "milk" as a metaphor for healthy, wise-love inspiration. We read his insights in *The Gospel of Thomas*, Saying 22:

Jesus
peered upon some little-ones
taking milk

And
he
said to his disciples:

"These little-ones
who
take milk[1]

They
are comparable
to those

Who
go inward
to the Kingdom."[2]

The disciples
responded:

"Then
we
being
little-ones

We
will go inward
to the Kingdom?"[3]

Jesus
responded:

"When
you
should make the two
the one[4]

[1] *Milk:* Healthy, complete, inspiration

[2] *These little-ones who take milk are comparable to those who go inward to the Kingdom:* These babes who drink inspiration are like Israelites who "go" inward to the Promised Earth.

[3] *Then we, being little ones, we will go inward to the Kingdom?* Then, we being Israelites who follow you (as the Israelites followed Moses), we are the little ones who will "go" into the Promised Earth?

[4] *Jesus responded:* "When you should make the two the one... Jesus responded: You need to do more than follow me around to be a little Israelite who drinks milk (inspiration) each moment. You cannot be one with Spirit's inspiration until you stop being "two;" that is until you stop being divided between your real and false selves.

> Then
> you
> will go inward
> to the Kingdom."[5]

> [5]*Then, you will go inward to the Kingdom."* Then, you will drink milk as a little Israelite child and "go inward" to the Promised Earth.

In this poem, Jesus teaches that an Israelite needs to "go" from their false identities to "go" to being guided by Spirit to the Promised Earth. When one does that, he leaves his pharaohs and becomes *one* with himself, not *two*.

BACK TO THE ALLEGORY

Would that we had died by the hand of Being in the land of Egypt when we sat by the cooking pots and when we ate bread until we were filled.

Cooking pots: Containers of dogma.

Bread: Wisdom. Here it is the so-called wisdom imposed by pharaohs.

Until we were filled: Until we Dogmaites became mind-dead secure in brainwashed dogma.

Being said to Moses: "Say to them, 'At twilight, you shall eat meat.'" Say to them, "When things begin to become difficult ("at twilight"), you will eat hard to digest (integrate) meat (wisdom).

Being said to Moses: "Say to them, 'In the morning you shall have your fill of bread.'" Say to them, "When you are not facing hard times ("in the morning" with the rising sun), you will eat inspired, easy-to-digest, Soul-Way bread (wisdom).

In the evening, quails came up and covered the camp; and in the morning, there was a layer of dew around the camp. When the layer of dew lifted, there on the surface of the wilderness was a fine, flaky substance, called "manna."

"Quails: "Meat" or wisdom. Meat is hard to digest because it confronts us with our false selves and their associated beliefs.

Dew: "Dew" is soft, encouraging inspiration.

"Manna:" It is easy-to-digest bread (wisdom) that supports us at a higher level of wise-love and truth.

When the Israelites saw it, they said to one another, "What is it?" For they did not know what it was. When the Israelites tasted manna (Soul-Way wisdom) for the first time, they did not even recognize it, because they have been feasting on spoiled bread (Mind-Way dogma) in Egypt all of their lives.

Moses said to them, "It is the bread that Being has given you to eat. The people shall go out and gather a day's portion every day.

A "day" is a moment of enlightenment when we know all with the Tree of the Knowledge of Life. The lyrics of a popular song express this experience, "On a clear day, you can see forever."

Gather a day's portion every day. You will continually "gather" wisdom for your use in the moment. You do not gather wisdom, and then, live for a period without obtaining more.

Moses said, "Gather as much of it as each of you needs… Let no one leave any of it over until morning." But they did not listen to Moses; some left part of it until morning, and it bred worms and became bad.

We are tempted to rely on yesterday's insights and not do the steps to obtain more "bread" (wisdom to evolve) today. When that happens, our wisdom becomes "bad," that is, it becomes dogma. We also become filled with "worms" (worry), because we have chosen to live in the past on the Mind Way.

Morning by morning they gathered it, each as much as he could eat. In easy times ("morning"), each person listened to Spirit and integrated what he heard.

But when the sun grew hot, it melted. When times were difficult (when the sun grew hot), they abandoned eating manna (life wisdom).

Being said to Moses, "How long will you refuse to keep my commandments and laws? Being said to Moses, "How long will you refuse both to live the Garden Command and the Covenant, and to circumcise yourself and sacrifice your Isaacs.

THE WILDERNESS OF SIN LESSONS

Spirit and Moses tried to teach the Israelites to rely on meat and bread wisdom in every moment. The people could do that in tranquil times; however, when difficulties arose, they reverted to their old Egyptian dogmas.

CHAPTER TWENTY-ONE

THE MOSES ALLEGORY: BEWARE OF THE LEADER WHO BECOMES A PHARAOH

We now learn how an exasperated Moses radically transforms his leadership of the people (Exodus 18:13-26):

It happened the next day that Moses sat to judge the people, and the people stood around him from morning till evening. When Moses' father-in-law saw all that he was doing for the people, he said, "What is this thing you are doing for the people? Why do you alone sit as a judge?"

Moses said to his father-in-law, "Because the people come to me to inquire of the Gods. When they have a dispute, it is brought to me, and I judge between a man and his neighbor, and make known Gods' decrees and laws."

Moses' father-in-law, Jethro, replied, "What you are doing is not good. You will wear out, both you and the people who are with you. The task is too heavy. You cannot do it alone. Listen. I will give you counsel...Select from all the people able men who fear the Gods, men of truth who hate dishonest gain, and appoint them over them as thousands, hundreds, fifties, and tens. They will judge the people at all times, but every major dispute the judges will bring to you, but every minor dispute they can decide."

So Moses heeded the voice of his father-in-law and did all that he had said.

The next day Moses took his seat to serve as a judge for the people, and they stood around him from morning till evening. The next day Moses relented to the complaining people and decided he would be a pharaoh who would tell them how to think and act.

The situation: Moses knows how to communicate with Spirit. The people do not want to learn to do that. Instead, they want a religious/political leader to tell them how to believe and behave.

What is Moses to do? He could abandon most of his Dogmaite people in the wilderness and lead only those who are true Israelites. Or, to keep order and his job, and out of false love, he could become a dark, controlling pharaoh. He chose the latter way.

Moses could have replied, "Look, my people. You need to discover your answers with the help of Spirit. In these past months, you would have learned to gather quail and manna as I instructed, you would not be in such emotional turmoil without direction. Sorry. For your sake, I will not indoctrinate you with my answers."

As the Israelites became more desperate for answers and more unwilling to go to Spirit for them, Moses chose the easy way to keep short-term peace: He became a controlling pharaoh.

When Moses' father-in-law saw all that Moses was doing for the people, he said, "What is this that you are doing for the people? Why do you alone sit as a judge?"

Moses' father-in-law is a Dogmaite. He approves of Moses becoming a cult leader; however, he wonders why Moses does not manage more efficiently by delegating some of his power to others.

Moses said to his father-in-law, "Because the people come to me to inquire of the Gods. When they have a dispute, it is brought to me, and I judge between a man and his neighbor and make known Gods' decrees and laws." Moses said to his father-in-law: "I judge alone because the people go only to me to tell them how to think and act. They believe that I am the only one who can communicate with the Gods."

Moses' father-in-law, Jethro, replied, "What you are doing is not good. You will wear out, both you and the people who are with you. The task is too heavy. You cannot do it alone. Listen. I will give you counsel…Select from all the people able men who fear God, men of truth who hate dishonest gain, and appoint them over them as thousands, hundreds, fifties, and tens. They will judge the people at all times, but every major dispute they (the judges) will bring to you, but every minor dispute they can decide."

Jethro wants Moses to not "wear himself out" by being the judge of everyone in every situation. So, he counsels Moses to establish a hierarchy of leaders who will judge according to standardized doctrine. In that way, Moses can create a theologically-based political system.

Moses listened to his father-in-law and did everything he said. So, Moses led people out from under the Egyptian Pharaoh to enslave them to him as another pharaoh.

PHARAOHS AND THEIR TASKMASTERS

Jesus speaks of indoctrinators like Moses and his hierarchy of judges critically in *The Gospel of Thomas* (Saying 102):

Woe to them
the Pharisees[1]

[1]*Pharisees:* Leaders who indoctrinate people rather than empower them to discover their wisdom with the help of Spirit.

For
they
resemble
a dog,[2]

[2]*Dog:* In ancient times, some people regarded dogs as the lowest of the low. They ate in the garbage dumps.

He
resting[3]
upon the manger[4]
of some oxen.[5]

[3]*Resting:* Not laboring to be guided by Spirit.

[4]*Manger:* The place within where we go to communicate in oneness with Spirit.

[5]*Oxen:* Brainwashed, stubborn Dogmaites.

For when
he
rests there

He
eats
not[6]

[6]*He eats not:* He does not communicate with Spirit.

And
he
permits
not the oxen
to eat.[7]

[7]*And He permits not the oxen to eat:* And the indoctrinating leader tells people that they cannot communicate directly with Spirit and must come to him for official answers.

Summary

The author of the Moses allegory has shown us, brilliantly, how well-meaning-but-weak leaders, like Moses, stop empowering people to be on the Soul Way, and instead, provide what the people think they want—a hierarchy of sub-pharaohs to control their thinking and behavior.

Moses has corrupted the Way of Abraham. These two leaders now oppose each other.

CHAPTER TWENTY-TWO

THE MOSES ALLEGORY: DON'T BOW TO PHARAOHS

Moses has chosen to be a Pharaoh. Now, to be in full control, he needs to make his followers afraid to question his authority.

Moses went up on the mountain and Being called to him and said, "I am going to come to you in a dense cloud so that the people will hear me speaking with you and will always put their trust in you...Put limits for the people around the mountain and tell them, 'Be careful that you do not approach the mountain or touch the foot of it, for whoever touches the mountain is to be put to death.'"

On the morning of the third day there was thunder and lightning, as well as a thick cloud on the mountain, and a blast of a trumpet so loud that all the people who were in the camp trembled. Moses brought the people out of the camp to meet Being. They took their stand at the foot of the mountain. Even the priests who approached the Lord consecrated themselves so that Being would not punish them. Exodus 19:9-22).

Moses went up on the mountain: A "mountain" is any place where one communicates with Spirit. It could be in one's bedroom or a beautiful garden.

Being called to him and said, "I am going to come to you in a dense cloud so that the people will hear me speaking with you and will always put their trust in you." A "dense cloud" is an illusion that makes Dogmaites "trust" a pharaoh's dogmas and those of the institution he represents.

Exercise

Questions for Reflection: Today, what do pharaohs do to put themselves in a "cloud" high above people to make them trust official dogmas? Please answer "yes" or "no" to the following statements:

1. They display and promote their titles.

2. They stand and speak high above others.

3. They build grand edifices that proclaim the sacredness and absolute truth of the doctrine spoken within.

4. They wear exotic, distinguishing clothing.

5. They wear symbols of authority.

6. They stand on tradition.

7. They punish dissent.

My answer: Pharaohs do all of those seven things.

Back to the Allegory

"Put limits for the people around the mountain." Find ways to convince people that they are not worthy of communicating directly with Spirit.

EXERCISE

QUESTIONS FOR REFLECTION: Today, what do pharaohs do to "put limits" on people so that they will not "go" to the "mountain" to communicate directly with Spirit? (Answer "yes" or "no" to the following options):

1. Encourage people to go to a place of retreat where they can communicate with Spirit without being influenced by others.

2. Establish seminaries to educate and ordain "holy" leaders who, unlike the un-ordained 1) have direct links to Spirit, 2) superior abilities to interpret scripture, and 3) special powers to lead rituals.

3. Host small discussion groups where people can tell each other what they have discovered when talking to Spirit.

4. Teach Soul Way principles, logic, and steps.

5. Tell people that scripture is their ultimate authority because it was composed by people who, unlike them, communicate with Spirit.

6. Establish "sacred" spaces where only "holy" leaders can go.

MY ANSWERS:

Today, what do pharaohs do to "put limits" on people going to the "mountain" to communicate directly with Spirit? (Answer "yes" or "no" to the following options):

1. Encourage people to go to a place of retreat where they can communicate with Spirit without being influenced by others. **My answer:** No

2. Establish seminaries to educate and ordain "holy" leaders who, unlike the unordained 1) have direct links to Spirit, 2) superior abilities to interpret scripture, and 3) special powers to lead rituals. **My answer:** Yes

3. Host small discussion groups where people can tell each other what they have discovered when talking to Spirit. **My answer:** No

4. Teach Soul Way principles, logic, and steps. **My answer:** No

5. Tell people that scripture is their ultimate authority because it was composed by people who, unlike them, communicate with Spirit. **My answer:** Yes

6. Establish "sacred" spaces where only "holy" leaders can go. **My answer:** Yes

Back to the Allegory

"And tell them, 'Be careful that you do not approach the mountain or touch the foot of it, for whoever touches the mountain is to be put to death.'"

Exercise:

Questions for Reflection: In which of the following ways do pharaohs sometimes punish people who get dissenting information directly from Spirit? (Answer "yes" or "no" to the following options):

1. When people dissent, they are told that they are perfect-as-is.

2. When people dissent, they are told that they are bad.

3. When people dissent, they are scorned and ostracized.

4. When people dissent, they are humiliated.

5. When people dissent, they are labeled as heretics.

6. When people dissent, they are denied privileges.

7. When people dissent, they are praised for standing up for what Spirit tells them.

8. When people dissent, they are tortured and killed.

My answers:

In which of the following ways do pharaohs sometimes punish people who get dissenting information directly from Spirit? (Answer "yes" or "no" to the following options):

1. When people dissent, they are told that they are perfect-as-is. **My answer:** No.

2. When people dissent, they are told that they are bad. **My answer:** Yes.

3. When people dissent, they are scorned and ostracized. **My answer:** Yes.

4. When people dissent, they are humiliated. **My answer:** Yes.

5. When people dissent, they are labeled as heretics. **My answer:** Yes.

6. When people dissent, they are denied privileges. **My answer:** Yes.

7. When people dissent, they are praised for standing up for what Spirit tells them. **My answer:** No.

8. When people dissent, they are marginalized, tortured, and killed. **My answer:** Yes.

Jesus in *The Gospel of Thomas* (Saying 39) explains powerfully how pharaohs prevent people from intimately communicating with God.

The Pharisees
and
the Scribes[1]
took the keys
of knowledge[2]

[1]*Pharisees and Scribes:* Indoctrinating leaders, whether religious or secular.

[2]*Keys of knowledge:* Soul Way principles, logic, and steps.

And
they
hid them[3]

[3]*Hid them:* Taught people that they needed to get personal information from ordained leaders.

Nor
did
they
go inward.[4]

[4]*Nor did they go inward:* Nor did they use the Soul Way to evolve in life.

And those
who
desire
to go inward

They
did
not permit them.[5]

[5]*They did not permit them:* The leaders taught the people to make official dogmas more important than anything they soul-sensed from Spirit.

You
however
come to be
cunning
like snakes[6]

[6]*Come to be cunning like snakes:* Grow to wisely move and work in the world of pharaohs and their followers without being part of it.

And
you
come to be
innocent
like doves.[7,8]

[7]*Innocent like doves:* Open, one with oneself, pure.

[8]*Come to be innocent and cunning:* Come to be wise-love of All.

BACK TO THE ALLEGORY

On the morning of the third day there was thunder and lightning, as well as a thick cloud on the mountain, and a blast of a trumpet so loud that all the people who were in the camp trembled. Moses brought the people out of the camp to meet the Gods. They took their stand at the foot of the mountain... Even the priests who approach Being must consecrate themselves, or Being will break out against them.

EXERCISE:

QUESTIONS FOR REFLECTION: Please answer, "yes or no" to the following: Does the tone and Spirit of the above paragraph:

1. Invite you to be intimate with Spirit?

2. Invite you to adore Spirit as totally other?

3. Invite you to be afraid of Spirit?

4. Invite you to have back and forth conversations with Spirit?

5. Remind you of a peaceful time you had talking to Spirit in a beautiful setting?

6. Remind you of a thundering organ in a grand cathedral where only special consecrated priests communicate with Spirit?

7. Invite you to be obedient to religious leaders?

8. Invite you to challenge religious leaders?

9. Invite you to see Moses as a pharaoh?

10. Invite you to see Moses as a person like you?

My answers:

Please answer, "yes or no" to the following: Does the tone and Spirit of the above paragraph:

1. Invite you to be intimate with Spirit? **My answer:** No.

2. Invite you to adore Spirit as totally other? **My answer:** Yes.

3. Invite you to be afraid of Spirit? **My answer:** Yes.

4. Invite you to have back and forth conversations with Spirit? **My answer:** No.

5. Remind you of a peaceful time you had talking to Spirit in a beautiful setting? **My answer:** No.

6. Remind you of a thundering organ in a grand cathedral where only special consecrated priests communicate with Spirit? **My answer:** Yes.

7. Invite you to be obedient to religious leaders? **My answer:** Yes.

8. Invite you to challenge religious leaders? **My answer:** No.

9. Invite you to see Moses as a pharaoh? **My answer:** Yes.

10. Invite you to see Moses as a person like you? **My answer:** No.

Summary

Moses	Eve, Abraham, Buddha, and Jesus
Makes himself a more important source of information than Spirit.	Makes Spirit the most important source of information (Buddha never mentions "Spirit").
Demands that we create false selves as we identify with his dogma.	Empowers us to be ourselves.
Punishes people who challenge established doctrine.	Encourages people to challenge established doctrine.
Stands above and apart from people.	Stands with people in oneness.
Demands respect.	Unconditionally loves people whether they return respect or not.
Founded the religion that we know as Judaism.	Led people out of religion and all other indoctrinating organizations

CHAPTER TWENTY-THREE

THE MOSES ALLEGORY: MAKE HUMAN LAWS SECONDARY TO NATURAL LAWS

THE SITUATION

Moses has founded a controlling religion by first, establishing a hierarchy of leaders subordinate to his rule; second, officially ordaining himself as Spirit's spokesperson; third, by terrifying everyone into submission to him and his version of Spirit, and fourth, by abrogating his responsibility to teach the Garden Command and the Covenant. Now, to complete his control over his followers, he must indoctrinate his lower-ranking pharaohs and followers with his absolutely true commandments and laws about how to think and act.

THE GENERAL TEN COMMANDMENTS

Moses went up on Mount Sinai. There, he obtained the Ten Commandments that he would proclaim as Spirit's general laws (Exodus 20:1-17). We see them in the chart below on the left. On the right, we see the Garden Command and the Covenant. Let us read the two sets of laws side-by-side and decide which lead to more death and which to more life.

THE TEN COMMANDMENTS	THE GARDEN COMMAN AND THE COVENANt
Do not bring other gods before my face.	Of the (fruit) of the Tree (of the Knowledge of Life) in the (middle of the) Garden of Eden take
Do not make for yourself an idol.	
Do not use the name of Being to build yourself up.	
Remember the Sabbath day.	And eat
Honor your father and your mother.	And eat;
Do not murder.	
Do not commit adultery.	Of the (fruit) of the Tree of the Knowledge of Good and Bad do not take
Do not steal.	
Do not make false witness against your neighbor.	
Do not covet…anything that is your neighbor's.	And eat
	And eat.
	For on the day you eat of it

You

will die

And

die."

———————•———————

Go from the land
of your tribe
and
your father's house

And
go to the earth

That
I
will show you....

EXERCISE:

QUESTIONS FOR REFLECTION: Concerning the above two sets of laws:

1. Which set of laws prescribes in detail how people are to think and act in specific situations?

2. Which set of laws frees people to decide for themselves how to think and act based on general principles one applies to every situation in every moment of every day?

3. Which set of laws is composed by a Dogmaite leader who wants to enslave his followers?

4. Which set of laws are natural to us (in our DNA) and which are human-made?

My answers:

1. Which set of laws prescribes in detail how people are to think and act in specific situations? **My answer:** Most of the Ten Commandments do that. However, it could be argued that the first two commandments ("Do not bring other gods before my face," and, "Do not make for yourself an idol") restate the part of the Covenant that says, "Go from the land of your tribes and your father's house").

2. Which set of laws frees people to decide for themselves how to think and act based on general principles one applies to every situation in every moment of every day? **My answer:** The Garden Command and the Covenant.

3. Which set of laws is composed by a Dogmaite leader who wants to enslave his followers? **My answer:** The Ten Commandments.

4. Which set of laws are natural to us (in our DNA) and which are human-made? **My answer:** The Garden Command and the Covenant.

Jesus and the Ten Commandments

In *The Gospel of Thomas* (Saying 27), Jesus explains the difference between living the Sabbath according to the Ten Commandments and according to the Covenant:

If
you
do
not make the Sabbath
outward[1]
the Sabbath
inward[2]

[1]*Sabbath outward:* A day of the week in which people devote some time to communicate with Spirit.

[2]*Sabbath inward:* A time when everything is secondary to continual communication with Spirit.

You
will peer[3]
not
upon the Father.[4]

[3]*Peer:* Third-eye see.

[4]*You will peer not upon the Father:* You will not continually experience Spirit in all.

In this poem, Jesus changes Moses' Commandment about observing the Sabbath at a specific time to the general Soul Way rule: be in the moment all day, every day being guided by Spirit to "go" to the Promised Earth. In that way, he showed how one of Moses' Commandments controls people and how Abraham's core principle frees them.

THE SPECIFIC TORAH LAWS

After Moses received the Ten Commandments up on Mount Sinai, he dictated over six hundred more specific laws about how people are to believe and behave. These have come to be called "Torah Laws." Some of them are:

When you buy a Hebrew slave, he shall serve six years, and in the seventh, he shall go out free. "If he comes in by himself, he shall go out by himself; if he comes in married, then his wife shall go out with him (Exod. 21:1-3).

When a man sells his daughter as a slave, she shall not go out as the male slaves do. If she does not please her master, who designated her for himself, then he shall let her be redeemed; he shall have no right to sell her to a foreign people since he has dealt unfairly with her. If he designates her for his son, he shall deal with her as with a daughter (Exod. 21:7-9).

If people fight and hit a pregnant woman, and she gives birth prematurely, but there is no serious injury, the offender must be fined whatever the woman's husband demands and the court allows. But if there is a serious injury, you are to take a life for a life, an eye for an eye, a tooth for a tooth, a hand for a hand, a foot for a foot, a burn for a burn, a wound for a wound, a bruise for a bruise (Exod. 21:21-25).

And you shall make an altar of shittim wood, five cubits long, and five cubits broad; the altar shall be foursquare: and the height of it shall be three cubits. And thou shalt make the horns of it upon the four corners: his horns shall be of the same: and you shall overlay it with brass (Exod. 27:1-6).

Do not dishonor your father by having sexual relations with your mother (Leviticus 18:7).

Three times in a year shall all thy males appear before Being in the place which he shall choose; in the feast of unleavened bread, and the feast of weeks, and the feast of tabernacles (Deut. 16:16).

If brothers dwell together, and one of them dies and has no son, the widow of the dead man shall not be married to a stranger outside the family; her husband's brother shall go in to her, take her as his wife, and perform the duty of a husband's brother to her (Deut. 25:5).

If a man is found kidnapping any of his brethren of the children of Israel, and mistreats him or sells him, then that kidnapper shall die; and you shall put away the evil from among you (Deut. 24:7).

When Being-Gods deliver your enemies over to you, you shall conquer them and utterly destroy them. You shall make no covenant with them nor show mercy to them. Nor shall you make marriages with them. You shall not give your daughter to their son, nor take their daughter for your son. For they will turn your sons away from following Me, to serve other gods; so the anger of Being will be aroused against you and destroy you suddenly. But thus you shall deal with them: you shall destroy their altars, and break down their sacred pillars, and cut down their wooden images, and burn their carved images with fire (Deut. 7:2-5).

And the swine, because it parts the hoof and is cloven-footed but does not chew the cud, is unclean to you (Lev. 11:7).

And you shall not glean your vineyard, nor shall you gather every grape of your vineyard; you shall leave them for the poor and the stranger (Lev. 19:10).

You shall not hate your brother in your heart. You shall surely rebuke your neighbor and not bear sin because of him (Lev. 19:17).

When you have eaten and are full, then you shall bless Being-Gods for the good land which has been given to you (Deut. 8:10).

If an ox gores a man or a woman to death, then the ox shall surely be stoned, and its flesh shall not be eaten; but the owner of the ox shall be acquitted (Exod. 21:28).

You shall neither mistreat a stranger nor oppress him, for you were strangers in the land of Egypt (Exod. 22:21).

A man or a woman who is a medium, or who has familiar spirits, shall surely be put to death; they shall stone them with stones. Their blood shall be upon them (Lev. 20:27).

You shall not let your livestock breed with another kind. You shall not sow your field with mixed descendants. Nor shall a garment of mixed linen and wool come upon you (Lev. 19:19).

A woman shall not wear anything that pertains to a man, nor shall a man put on a woman's garment (Deut. 22:5).

Jesus' Response to Moses' Commandments and Laws

At one point in Jesus' ministry, his disciples wondered if he followed Moses. Here is how Jesus responded (*The Gospel of Thomas*, Saying 6):

Jesus' disciples
asked him:

"Do
you
want

That
we
fast?

And
what
is
the manner

That
we
will pray?

And
shall we
abstain
from certain foods?"

And
shall we
give alms?[1]

Jesus
responded:

"You
do
not speak lies.[2]

And
what
you
hate in him[3]

[1] By these questions, the disciples ask Jesus if they need to follow the Ten Commandments and the Torah Laws to live in the Kingdom.

[2] *You do not speak lies:* Do not lie by saying you are of value because you live Moses' dogmas. Instead, honestly value yourself for being the divine life in you and everyone.

[3] *What you hate in him:* What we hate in anyone is lying. That happens when someone knows himself as "bad" and covers up his perfect-as-is real selves with garments (false selves).

You do not do to him;[4]	[4]*What you hate in him, you do not do to him:* When you see someone who sees himself as "bad," do not know him as "bad."
For they are revealed	
All of them In the presence of heaven."[5]	[5]*For they are revealed …in the presence of heaven:* For another's falseness will be revealed when confronted by someone living a high level of wisdom and love.

In the above poem, Jesus' disciples wanted to know they are good and that others are bad. They think they can do that by identifying with Moses' commandments and laws. Jesus will have none of that. Instead, he says that if you want to "reveal" and correct what is bad, "reveal" yourself to be full of life. You do that by knowing yourself and others with the Tree of the Knowledge of Life. Then, you will be a light savior in the dark world.

EXERCISE:

QUESTIONS FOR REFLECTION:

1. Which tree of knowledge did Abraham use when he listened for laws from Spirit?

2. Which tree of knowledge did Moses use when he listened for laws from Spirit?

MY ANSWERS:

1. Which tree of knowledge did Abraham use when he listened for laws from Spirit? **My answer:** The Tree of the Knowledge of Life.

2. Which tree of knowledge did Moses use when he listened for laws from Spirit? **My answer:** The Tree of the Knowledge of Good and Bad. Like all cult leaders, Moses controlled followers by telling them when they were good and when they were bad. When he declared, "Do not bring other gods before my face" and, "Do not make for yourself an idol," in essence, he said, "Do not worship anyone but me as the spokesperson for Spirit."

EXERCISE:

QUESTIONS FOR REFLECTION:

1. Do the Torah (and other religious) Laws restrict or free people?

2. Do the Torah (and other religious) Laws encourage people to be one with Spirit guidance or one with Moses' guidance?

3. Will the Torah (and other religious) Laws enable people to enter the Promised Earth?

4. Would you prefer to focus all day, every day, on observing the Ten Commandments and the Torah (and other religious) Laws or on keeping the Garden Command and the Covenant? Why?

MY ANSWERS:

1. Do the Torah (and other religious) Laws restrict or free people? **My answer:** They intend to control people.

2. Do the Torah (and other religious) Laws encourage people to be one with Spirit guidance or with Moses' guidance? **My answer:** Moses' guidance.

3. Will the Torah (and other religious) Laws enable people to enter the Promised Earth? **My answer:** When one makes the observance of the Torah (and other religious) Laws more important than being guided by Spirit, he violates the Covenant. Therefore, he would be blocked from entering the Promised Earth.

4. Would you prefer to focus all day, every day, on observing the Ten Commandments and the Torah (and other religious) Laws or on keeping the Garden Command and the Covenant? Why? **My answer:** I would become a self-absorbed, neurotic robot if I focused all day, every day on the observance of the Ten Commandments and the Torah (and other religious) Laws. The Garden Command and the Covenant free me to be one with Spirit guidance.

SUMMARY

As we choose our commandments and laws, we choose our lives:

DOGMAITES	ISRAELITES
Live detailed commandments and laws that tell them how to believe and behave in specific situations.	Live general commandments and laws that tell them to use Spirit guidance to be wise-love of All in any situation.
Judge themselves as "good" when they observe specific commandments and laws, and others as "bad" when they do not.	They wise-love All no matter what commandments and laws they observe.
They become enslaved robots.	They become free individualists.

CHAPTER TWENTY-FOUR

THE MOSES ALLEGORY: BEWARE OF RELIGIOUS TYRANTS

When Moses was up on Mt. Sinai obtaining the Ten Commandments and the Torah Laws, his people rebelled:

When the people saw that Moses delayed to come down from the mountain, the people gathered themselves together to Aaron (Moses' brother) and said to him, "Up, make us gods who shall go before us. As for this Moses, the man who brought us up out of the land of Egypt, we do not know what has become of him."

And Aaron said to them, "Take off the rings of gold which are in the ears of your wives, your sons, and your daughters, and bring them to me." So, all the people took off the rings of gold which were in their ears and brought them to Aaron. And he received the gold from their hand, and fashioned it with a graving tool, and made a molten calf, and he said, "This is your god, O Israel, who brought you up out of the land of Egypt"....

And Being said to Moses, "Go down; for your people, whom you brought up out of the land of Egypt, have corrupted themselves...now, therefore, let me alone, that my wrath may burn hot against them and I may consume them...

And as soon as Moses came near the camp and saw the calf and the dancing, his anger burned hot, and he threw the tablets (of the Ten Commandments) out of his hands and broke them at the foot of the mountain...

Then Moses stood in the gate of the camp, and said, "Who is on Being's side? Come to me."

And all the sons of Levi gathered themselves together to him.

And he said to them, "Thus says The Being-Gods of Israel, 'Every man put his sword on his side, and go to and fro from gate to gate throughout the camp, and slay every man and his brother, and every man and his companion, and every man and his neighbor.'"

And the sons of Levi did according to the word of Moses. Thus, there fell of the people that day about three thousand men.

Then Moses said, "You have been set apart for Being today, for you were against your own sons and brothers, and he has blessed you this day." (Exod. 32:1-29)

When the people saw that Moses delayed to come down from the mountain, they gathered themselves together to Aaron, and said to him, "Up, make us Gods who shall go before us; as for this Moses, the man who brought us up out of the land of Egypt, we do not know what has become of him." The people said to Aaron (Moses' brother), "Up, make us gods who will provide us with all of our answers. We cannot wait for Moses to return to tell us how to think and act. Further, we do not want to learn how to use Spirit Guidance to make our own decisions."

And Aaron said to them, "Take off the rings of gold which are in the ears of your wives, your sons, and your daughters, and bring them to me." So, all the people took off the rings of gold which were in their ears and brought them to Aaron.

"Gold" symbolizes our most precious possessions and the beliefs about them that support our false selves.

And Aaron received the gold from their hand, and fashioned it with a graving tool and made a molten calf. And he took their valuable possessions and their associated dogmas and made them into an idol to be worshiped as their savior.

When we make an idol of "gold," we choose to adore our most precious possession rather than Spirit as our savior. This happens automatically to us when we worship our money, nation, faith, possessions, and friends as the things that save us. So, in each moment, we either meltdown our gold to make idols, or we choose to "go" from them to use Spirit to "go" to the Promised Earth.

For example, if one's family is one's "gold," then one makes an idol out of his family. That false god must be destroyed to be one with Spirit. To do that, one must de-identify from his family. One way to do that is to follow Spirit even when to do so upsets the family.

Or, in another example, if one's faith is one's "gold," then one makes idols out of those blind beliefs. Those false gods must be destroyed so that one can be one with Spirit. To do that, one must de-identify from his dogmas. One can do that by making all dogmas less important than third-eye and ear communicating with Spirit.

And Aaron said, "This is your god, O Israel, who brought you up out of the land of Egypt." This is your ego and its beliefs, O Israel, and not Spirit, that brought you up out of Egyptian religious and political enslavement.

And Being said to Moses, "Go down; for your people whom you brought up out of the land of Egypt have corrupted themselves. And Moses' version of Spirit said, "Moses, Go down, for your people who you brought out of Egyptian mind control have corrupted themselves by not worshiping you and your dogmas. Instead, they have invented another religion.

Being said, "Now, therefore, let me alone, that my wrath may burn hot against them and I may consume them. And Moses' bad-good version of Spirit said, "Let me punish them, and in the process, destroy their desire to be independent of you, Moses."

And as soon as Moses came near the camp and saw the calf and the dancing, his anger burned hot, and he threw the tablets (of the Ten Commandments) out of his hands and broke them at the foot of the mountain. As soon as Moses saw that his Dogmaites had disobeyed him, he became self-absorbed and angry. Then, he "broke" Commandments by setting himself over his people as a pharaoh who judges them as "bad" and himself as "good."

Moses stood in the gate of the camp and said, "Who is on Being's side? Come to me." Moses took a stand before the people and said, "Who is on *my* side as I interpret Spirit's love and wisdom? Come forth so I can determine who are my friends and who are my enemies."

And all the sons of Levi gathered themselves together to him. All of the descendants of Levi, the great Israelite priest, corrupted themselves by joining with Moses.

And he said to them, "Thus says The Being-Gods of Israel, 'Every man put his sword on his side, and go to and fro from gate to gate throughout the camp, and slay every man and his brother, and every man and his companion, and every man and his neighbor.'" And Moses said to his corrupted followers: "Spirit has told me to tell you to punish everyone who does not conform to my Ten Commandments and Torah Laws."

And the sons of Levi did according to the word of Moses. And there fell of the people that day about three thousand men.

Thousand: Metaphorically, a large number. So, "three thousand men" could mean 30 of a group of 100 or 30 thousand of a nation of 100,000.

The sons of Levi wiped out the "bad," rebellious Dogmaites to preserve the "good" Dogmaite religion of Moses.

Then Moses said, "You have been set apart for Being today, for you were against your own sons and brothers, and he has blessed you this day." Then Moses said, "My version of Spirit rewards you for psychologically and physically punishing people who disagree with my doctrine."

SUMMARY

Moses went up on his mountain, received inspired answers, declared those answers to be absolute truths, and rewarded those who believed and lived those truths, and punished those who do not.

CHAPTER TWENTY-FIVE

THE MOSES ALLEGORY: WE ARE PUNISHED AND REWARDED EVERY MOMENT

In three passages from Deuteronomy, we learn what happened to Moses and his people because they did or did not live Abraham's Covenant:

> *Being declared: Not one of these men of this evil generation shall see that good earth which I swore to give to your fathers... Even you, Moses, shall not go in there (Deut. 1:34-35).*

> *Joshua, the son of Nun, who stands before you, he shall go in there. Encourage him, for he shall cause Israel to inherit it (Deut.1:38).*

> *Ascend Mount Nebo...and view the earth, which I give to the children of Israel as a possession. There, you will die and be gathered to your people, because you broke faith with me amid the people of Israel at the waters of Marah and in the wilderness of Sin (Deut. 32: 49-51).*

Being declared: "Not one of these men of this evil generation shall see that good earth which I swore to give to your fathers. Even you, Moses, shall not go in there."

Generation: People from a common parentage.

Evil generation: Dogmaites. People who follow an indoctrinating pharaoh who entraps people on the Mind Way.

Being declared: "Not one of these men of this evil generation shall see that good earth of which I swore to give to your fathers." Not one of your followers, Moses, shall enter the earth that I promised to give to your fathers who were living the Covenant.

Even you, Moses, shall not go in there. Even you, Moses, who at one time communicated with Me, shall not live in the Promised Earth.

Joshua, the son of Nun, who stands before you, he shall go in there. Encourage him, for he shall cause Israel to inherit it. Joshua, who did not follow you, Moses, and instead learned to be guided by only Me, he shall enter the Promised Earth. Encourage and do not prevent him, for he shall teach Israelites how to "go" from pharaohs to "go" to an independent, fulfilled life.

———————◆●——————

Jesus, in *The Gospel of Thomas*, Poem 27, explains what Joshua did and what we must do to live in the Promised Earth:

<table>
<tr><td>If
you
do
not fast from the world[1]</td><td>[1]*If you do not fast from the world:* If you do not remove yourself from Dogmaites who do not make Spirit their primary leader…</td></tr>
<tr><td>You
will discover
not
the Kingdom.[2]</td><td>[2]*You will discover not the Kingdom:* You will not be led to discover the principles and logic for living in the Promised Earth.</td></tr>
</table>

———————◆●——————

Being said, "Moses, ascend Mount Nebo and view the earth which I give to the children of Israel as a possession." Moses, go up on your inner mountain and get a sense of the Light Experience, which I will give to the Israelites.

There on Mount Nebo, you will die and be gathered to your people. There, communicating with me on your mountain, you will die in the Dark Experience and be held in esteem by your Dogmaite followers.

You will die... because you broke faith with me amid the people of Israel at the waters of Marah and in the wilderness of Sin.

At the waters of Marah, in the wilderness of Sin, and in other locations, Moses kept faith with a people who did not choose to make Spirit their primary guide. He could have abandoned most and led only those Israelites like Joshua. But, out of false love, he established the comfortable, controlling religion that they sought.

Joshua explains the situation in Joshua 5:6:

For the sons of Israel walked forty years in the wilderness, until all the nation, the men of war that came forth out of Egypt, perished because they did not listen to the voice of Being.

Forty years: A long time, not forty actual years.

For the sons of Israel walked forty years in the wilderness: For the potential Israelites spent a long time wandering with only Moses' guidance. They left the control of the Egyptian Pharaoh, but because they did not use Spirit as their guide consistently, they were without moment-by-moment inspiration (water) in the "wilderness."

Until all the nation, the men of war that came forth out of Egypt perished.

Nation: Those on the Mind Way.

Men of war: To the degree that we are on the Mind Way, we are automatically at "war" with first, anyone who identifies with dogmas that differ from ours; and second, with ourselves, because we are divided between our real selves and our false selves. Unless we "go" from nations of Dogmaites and "go" forth on the Soul Way, we will live a slow, psychological death in one or more controlling organizations.

Summary

Peacemakers who identify with nothing but the divine life in themselves and others.

↑

War-mongers who identify with dogmas that divide us.

CHAPTER TWENTY-SIX

THE JOSHUA ALLEGORY: FOLLOW JOSHUA

After Moses died, Joshua led the Israelites to the Jordan River, which separated the wilderness from the Promised Earth:

Early in the morning, Joshua rose and came to the Jordan, and he and the people lodged there before they passed over.

At the beginning of the Light Experience ("early in the morning"), Joshua left ("rose") from Moses' dark environment and faced his emotions ("came to the Jordan") that were attached to his former dogmas. He and his followers pondered how to "pass over" their river of upset.

And Joshua said to the priests, "Take up the ark of the covenant and pass on before the people." And they took up the ark of the covenant and went before the people... And when their feet were dipped in the water, the water coming down from above stood and rose up in a heap far off...and the people passed over opposite Jericho on dry earth (Josh. 3:1-17).

Joshua said to the priests: "Take the ark of the covenant and pass over ahead of the people."

Ark: There are two Hebrew words for "ark" in the Bible. Tebah and Ärōn. Tebah means "ark" or "boat." That is the word used in the Noah allegory in Genesis. Ärōn means ark or chest. That is the word used here in the Joshua allegory.

Ark of the Covenant: A chest containing the Covenant. Metaphorically, the "ark" is one's heart which contains the Covenant. Everyone has such an ark; however, few are aware of its contents.

Joshua said to the Priests: "Take the ark of the Covenant and pass over ahead of the people." Joshua said to his leaders: "Live the Covenant. When you do that, you will teach the Israelites how to conquer their Jordan River of fear of "going" from their dogmas to "go" with Spirit guidance to the Promised Earth.

And when their feet were dipped in the water, the water coming down from above stood and rose up in a heap far off. And when they courageously confronted their emotions ("their feet dipped in the water") by living the Covenant without doubt, their wild upset did not disturb them.

And the people passed over on dry earth.

Dry earth: Joshua and his people like Moses and his people passed over on "dry earth," that is, on receptive, reflective consciousness that was not distracted (made wet) by emotions.

Passing over Water

There were similar ancient metaphors for confronting and conquering one's emotional attachments to people and things and their associated dogmas. All of them meant to "pass over" water. These metaphors included walking on water, dividing water, calming water, and building a boat to float on water.

There follows examples from the Bible and from the Dhammapada of "passing over water." For example:

EXODUS 14:21	JOSH. 3:1-17
Moses stretched out his hand over the sea. Then, Being drove the sea back by a strong east wind all night and made the **dry earth**. As a result, the waters were divided. Then Moses led Israel onward.	And when their feet were dipped in the water, the water coming down from above stood and rose up in a heap far off. And the people passed over opposite Jericho on **dry earth**.
GEN. 8:1-13	DHAMMAPADA (CH. 25)
And the Gods made a wind to pass over the earth and the waters retreated...	O' slave of desire float upon the streams. Seeker! empty the boat lighten the load of desires and passions.

And
Noah
removed the covering
of the ark
and looked,
and behold,
the face
of the **earth**
was **dry**.

Go beyond this Way
to the other side
where
the world dissolves
and
everything
becomes clear.

MATT. 14:25

MARK 4:39

And
in the fourth watch
of the night
Jesus
came to them
walking on the sea.

And
having raised himself
Jesus
rebuked the wind

And
said to the sea,

"Be silent!

Be muzzled!"

And
the wind
abated,

And
there
came to be a great calm.

In the above passages, we observe six of many instances in ancient literature where allegories describe metaphorically the process of personal evolution from a lower level of truth and love to a higher one. In each instance, a person needed to confront his distracting, controlling "sea" or "river" of emotions. He conquered them by living the Covenant in his Ark (heart).

The Israelite Conquest of the Promised Earth

After entering the Promised Earth, Joshua and his people conquered the various Dogmaite tribes who live there and who worship false gods (Josh. 12:7-10).

> *These are the kings of the land whom Joshua and the people of Israel defeated on the west side of the Jordan...the king of Jericho...the king of Jerusalem...(a long list of kings).*

These are the kings of the land whom Joshua and the people of Israel defeated on the west side of the Jordan...the king of Jericho...the king of Jerusalem...(a long list of kings). These are the pharaohs that the Israelites defeated.

———————◆———————

We are reading an allegory. The pharaohs that Joshua defeated are theologians, clergy, and other secular dogma indoctrinators. Israelites defeat such Mind Way "kings" and establish the Soul Way kingdom. Jesus describes this process in *The Gospel of Thomas*, Saying 113:

Jesus' disciples asked him:

"The Kingdom,[1]

It

is coming

It

on which day?"[2]

Jesus responded:

"The kingdom[3]

[1]*Kingdom:* The meaning of the word "Kingdom" is not the same for the disciples as it is for Jesus. The "Kingdom" for them is a physical Jewish country that will exist after the Messiah drives out the Romans. It will be patterned after the one ruled by King David (Dan. 8:17-19).

[2]*The Kingdom is coming on which day?* The disciples wanted to know when the Messiah would fulfill the prophesies that he would cleanse the temple of false teachings and bring everyone on earth into one physical government and into the worship the one true God (Is. 2:4; 9:5-10; Mal. 3:2; 4 Ezra 7:113; Zach. 6:13; Ezek. 37:21-24).

[3]*Kingdom:* The Light Experience. In it, one rules as a king or queen over himself and his interactions with others.

It
comes
not in watching[4]

They
will say
not this:
'Behold here

Or
behold there.'

Rather
the Kingdom
of the Father[5]

It
is spreading
upon the earth[6]

And
men[7]
peer
not upon it.

[4] *It comes not in watching:* The Kingdom will not come because you disciples stand around watching for what you cannot recognize until you live on the Soul Way.

[5] *Kingdom of the Father:* The way our Father lives. As one grows on the Soul Way, one lives more like Him.

[6] *Earth:* The reflective, receptive consciousness possessed by people on the Soul Way.

[7] *And men peer not upon it:* And Dogmaite men and women like you disciples cannot see the Kingdom because you do not live in it.

We see in this poem that the disciples were just like many today who think that the Messiah will establish a physical Kingdom. Instead, Jesus described a personal and global Kingdom under the rule of Spirit.

Joshua's Reign

As Joshua and his army conquered kingdoms in Canaan, he gave each of the twelve tribes a piece of territory. Then, there was a long period of peace. We read what happened next in the last paragraph of the Book of Joshua:

A long-time after Being had given rest to Israel from the enemies around them, Joshua became old. He then called all

Israelites to him...and said, "This day I am going the way of all on the land. You know in your hearts and souls that not one thing has failed of all the good things which Being-Gods predicted. Therefore, it shall come to pass that as Being gave you the promised good things; so also, Being can bring evil things upon you until he has destroyed you from off of this good earth which Being-Gods has given to you. But, this will only happen if you set aside the Covenant of Being-Gods which he commanded you to observe, and have gone and served other gods, and bowed to them. Then, shall the anger of Being burn and you shall perish quickly from off the good earth which he has given you (Josh. 23:14-16).

Joshua called all Israelites to him, and said, "This day I am going the way of all on the land. Just before dying, Joshua called the Israelites to him and said, "This day, I am going to die physically as does everyone."

Joshua said, "You know in your hearts and souls that not one thing has failed of all the good things which Being-Gods predicted." Joshua said: "Your third-eye and ear know that Spirit has guided you to what you most deeply desired."

Therefore, it shall come to pass that as Being gave you the promised good things; so also, Being can bring evil things upon you until he has destroyed you from off of this good earth which Being-Gods has given to you. Therefore, know that you are moment-by-moment on trial. Be aware that as Spirit has guided you to an evolved, higher level of life, Spirit also can guide you to a lower level of death if that is what you desire.

Joshua said, "But this only will happen if you set aside the Covenant of Being-Gods which he commanded you to observe, and have gone and served other gods, and bowed to them. Then, shall the anger of Being burn and you shall perish quickly from off the good earth which he has given you. Joshua said, "But, you will 'go' *from* the Promised Earth if you 'go' back to adoring idols (false selves) and following pharaohs rather than using Spirit to discover your own answers.

Joshua said: "Choose for yourselves this day whom you will serve, whether the gods which your fathers served that were on the other side of the River or the gods of the Amorites in whose land you dwell. But as for me and my house, we will serve Being."

So the people answered and said: "Far be it from us that we should forsake Being to serve other gods" (Josh. 24:15-16).

Joshua said, "Choose for yourselves this day whom you will serve." Joshua said, "Unlike Moses, I set you free to decide if you will serve pharaohs or Spirit."

So the people answered and said: "Far be it from us that we should forsake Being to serve other gods." The people responded to Joshua: "We will follow Spirit and not theological and secular pharaohs."

THE ISRAELITE GOLDEN AGE

We learn in the Book of Judges that after Joshua died, the Israelites lived for about 200 years in relative peace. In that book, the author never mentions the Torah Laws.[14] The Israelites followed Spirit, not pharaohs as we read in passages such as the following (Judges 17:6, 18:1, 19:1, and 21:25):

In those days, there was no king in Israel; everyone did what was right in his own eyes." (Judges 17:6, 18:1, 19:1, and 21:25).

In those days, there was no king in Israel; everyone did what was right in his own eyes. In those days, there was no scripture or pharaoh (theologian, clergy person, politician, commentator, or another kind of indoctrinator) enslaving the Israelites. Instead, the direct revelations from Spirit guided them.

The Israelites were not leaderless. Highly enlightened "judges" emerged in each community to facilitate people both to learn the Soul Way and to resolve differences. When the twelve Israelite

---

14   See Appendix Three.

tribes needed to unite against a common enemy, they selected one commanding judge to lead them — the Book of Judges names many, including the woman, Deborah. After the crisis ended, the unifying judge returned to his or her life as a local judge.

SUMMARY

Today, people all over the world, in every culture and from every walk of life have discovered the Soul Way. These individuals automatically bring disruption to Dogmaites, as did Joshua and his people. They are what Jesus called in Saying 32 in *The Gospel of Thomas*, "a city" "built upon a mountain."

A city[1]
is being built
upon a mountain[2]

It
raised[3]

It
fortified.[4]

In no way
might
it
fall[5]

Nor
can
it
be hidden.[6]

[1]*City:* A group of houses. A "house" is either a person with many rooms (false selves) or an "empty" house with no false selves.

[2]*A city is being built upon a mountain:* A person or community is being created as a world-wide "city" by Spirit who communicates with them on their inner mountain.

[3]*It raised:* It (the city) has been raised by Spirit over Dogmaites.

[4]*It fortified:* It (the city) guards itself against the influence of those living in darkness.

[5]*In no way might it fall:* In cannot be overthrown by Dogmaites.

[6]*Nor can it be hidden:* Nor can Dogmaites ignore the Israelite disruptions to their Mind Way.

In this Poem, Jesus describes the Israelite Golden Age. It was one giant "city built upon a mountain." As such, it was a disrupting, highly visible light to the dark world. It was also, perhaps, the last time the world experienced a large community of independent, wise-loving, united people.

CHAPTER TWENTY-SEVEN

THE SAUL AND DAVID ALLEGORY: DO NOT DIVIDE YOUR LOYALTIES

The Israelite Golden Age slowly deteriorated. Over time, the Israelites became the minority and the Dogmaites the majority. 1Sam. 3:1 describes this situation:

In those days, the word of Being was rare; there were not many visions.

In those days, fewer and fewer people made Spirit their primary guide.

As the Israelite Golden Age dwindled, Spirit raised Samuel as an Israelite judge to lead them: *"And all Israel from Dan to Beersheba recognized that Samuel was affirmed as a prophet of Being"* (1Sam. 3:19).

In 1Sam. 8:4-20, we read about how the Israelite golden age ended:

All the elders of Israel gathered together and came to Samuel at Ramah. They said to him, "You are old, and your sons do not follow your Way; now appoint a king to lead us, such as all the other nations have."

This displeased Samuel; so he prayed to Being. And Being told him: "Listen to all that the people are saying to you. It is not you they have rejected, but they have rejected me as their King as they have done from the day I brought them up out of Egypt until this day, forsaking me and serving other gods. In this way, they are doing the same to you. Now, listen to them; but warn them solemnly and of the procedure of the king who will reign over them."

Samuel told all the words of Being to the people who were asking him for a king. He said, "This is how the king will reign over you: You will become his slaves."

But the people refused to listen to Samuel. "No!" they said. "We want a king over us. Then we will be like all the other nations, with a king to lead us and to go out before us and fight our battles."

When Samuel heard all that the people said, he repeated it before Being. Being answered, "Listen to them and give them a king."

So all the elders of Israel gathered together and came to Samuel at Ramah. They said to him, "You are old, and your sons do not follow your Way; now appoint a king to lead us, such as all the other nations have." So all the elders abandoned their Israelite heritage and said to Samuel, the prophet, "You will die soon. Your immediate descendants do not follow the Soul Way any longer. Therefore, appoint a pharaoh to lead us so that we can be like other Dogmaite nations on the Mind Way."

This displeased Samuel; so he prayed to Being. Samuel did not want to abandon the Israelite tradition; so, he went apart upon his "mountain," became still and one with all, and communicated with Spirit.

Being told Samuel: "Listen to all that the people are saying to you. It is not you they have rejected, but they have rejected me as their king as they have done from the day I brought them up out of Egypt until this day, forsaking me and serving other gods. In this way, they are doing the same to you." And Spirit told Samuel: "Respectfully, listen to these Dogmaite leaders who have abandoned the Israelite minority. They are like the followers of Moses who refused to make Me their only guide. You, Samuel, are Me in their presence. So when they reject you, they reject Me."

The Saul and David Allegory: Do not Divide Your Loyalties 251

Being told Samuel, "Listen to them; but warn them solemnly of the procedure of the king who will reign over them." Spirit told Samuel: "Remind these Dogmaite leaders about how Moses and other pharaohs use manipulative tricks to control their thinking and behavior."

Samuel told the people who were asking him for a king, "This is how the king will reign over you: You yourselves will become his slaves." Samuel told the people: "This is how a pharaoh will reign over you: You will think that you have found independence, but in fact, you will pay in money and in loss of integrity to be a slave to his dogmas."

"No!" They said. "We want a king over us. Then we will be like all the other nations, with a king to lead us and to go out before us and fight our battles." "No," they said. "We do not want to be responsible for ourselves by communicating with Spirit. We want a pharaoh-king both to tell us how to live and to lead us in a battle."

The Situation

During the Israelite Golden Age, most of the people lived the Covenant and made Spirit their king. Gradually individuals and groups of people, each espousing their own set of dogmas, infiltrated the twelve tribes. As a result, the Kingdom became weak because each Dogmaite group judged itself as "good," and others with different dogmas, as "bad." That caused division between individuals and groups. Therefore, the leaders wanted a strong king who would impose secular laws on everyone and ensure that no individual or group attacked another.

Back to the Allegory

When Samuel heard all that the people said, he repeated it before Being. Being answered, "Listen to them and give them a king." Spirit reminded Samuel that to live the Covenant, he must permit people to be responsible for themselves and to live the consequences. If they want a pharaoh-king to lead them around by their unconscious, terrified noses, let them have such a leader.

Samuel Chooses Saul as King

Samuel needs the guidance of Spirit to find a person who would be such a strong king that he would both be able to force one set of laws on everyone and, at the same time, establish a pluralistic society in which people would be allowed to pursue their own dogmas.

> *There was a man of the tribe of Benjamin whose name was Kish, who had a special son, whose name was Saul. There was not a more handsome person than he among the children of Israel. He was taller than any of the people.*

> *When Samuel saw Saul, Being said to him, "There is the man of whom I spoke to you. He shall reign over My people" (1Sam. 9:1-17).*

> *Then Samuel took a flask of olive oil and poured it on Saul's head and kissed him, saying, "Has not Being anointed you ruler over his inheritance?"*

> *Samuel said to all the people, "Do you see the man that Being has chosen? There is no one like him among all the people." Then the people shouted, "Long live the king!" Then Samuel dismissed the people to go to their own homes.*

> *Saul also went to his home in Gibeah, accompanied by valiant men whose hearts the Gods had touched. But some rebels said, "How can this man save us?" So, they despised him and brought him no gifts. But Saul kept silent (1Sam. 10:1-27).*

There was not a more handsome person than Saul among the children of Israel... He was taller than any of the people. Spirit chose Saul as a leader who would be accepted and feared by the people because of his appearance and height, not because of his character.

Saul went to his home in Gibeah, accompanied by valiant men whose hearts the Gods had touched. After accepting his role as king of a divided Israel, Saul returned to his house accompanied by Israelites whom he favored.

But some rebels said, "How can this man save us?" So, they despised him and brought him no gifts. But some of the Dogmaites said, "How can this Israelite who does not embrace our dogmas protect us from other Dogmaites?" So, they despised him and caused division within the kingdom.

But Saul kept silent. But when Saul did not respond strongly with wise-love to this rebellion, he showed that he was a weak leader.

Exercise:

A Question for Reflection: Imagine that you are a king, like Saul, standing on a knoll overlooking a large field filled with the people in your kingdom. The majority are Dogmaites, each group of them promoting and defending a different set of dogmas. You see, for example, Buddhists, Christians, Muslims, Hindus, nationalists, racists, liberals, conservatives, etc.—each group of people thinking that they know the true way that everyone should live. Finally, you become aware of the burden placed on you, the King, because every person wants you to agree with his way of living his dogmas.

Then, over there off to the side of the field, you notice that 2% of the people are Israelites who do not identify with any religious, political, race, class, or other dogmas. They are faithful primarily to Spirit as their guide for living the Garden Command and the Covenant.

A Question for Reflection: If you were Saul, which of the following strategies will you use to bring about unity and peace in your kingdom?

1. Would you enable everyone to vote for those who would advise you even though most will be Dogmaites?

2. Would you give a speech imploring people to be tolerant of others who differ from them?

3. Would you tell everyone that you will punish anyone who does not get along peacefully with people with different dogmas or with Israelites who possess no dogma affiliation?

4. Would you write a constitution that gives everyone the right to free speech and free practice of their dogma-based religion? (This would include giving them the right to indoctrinate everyone else with their truths and to call those who agree with their dogmas, "bad").

5. Would you tell each group what they want to hear to make them think you agree with their dogmas?

6. Would you bring the leaders of every Dogmaite group together and demand that they agree on one set of dogmas for everyone?

7. Would you outlaw Dogmaite groups?

8. Would you force everyone to be an Israelite?

9. Would you lead:

    a. By being one with Spirit guidance,

    b. By modeling how you identify and sacrifice your Isaacs (false selves) daily,

    c. By wise-loving all with the Tree of the Knowledge of Life,

    d. By raising leaders who will teach both the Soul Way and the dangers inherent in living the Mind Way,

    e. By both listening respectfully to Dogmaite leaders and by explaining to them why you will not impose their dogmas on others,

    f. By ensuring that there is no direct or indirect government support of Dogmaite groups, and

    g. By selecting an Israelite cabinet to advise and monitor you?

MY ANSWER: I favor all of number nine, which was operative during the Israelite golden age. All of the other methods will not stop division within a kingdom.

Back to the Allegory

So Saul established his sovereignty over Israel, and fought against all his enemies on every side, against Moab, against the people of Ammon, against Edom, against the kings of Zobah, and the Philistines 1Sam. 14:47).

Saul fought continuously with everyone. When one Dogmaite group tried to impose its doctrine on everyone else, he gathered the other groups in his kingdom and put down the rebellion. When an outside group attacked, he united his people against them.

Now, because Spirit noticed that deep down, Saul did not realize the danger of Dogmaites, he told Samuel what to say to Saul:

Samuel said to Saul, "Now, therefore, listen to the voice of the words of Being. 'I will punish Amalekites for what they did to Israel, how they ambushed them on their way up from Egypt. Now go and attack the Amalekites and utterly destroy them. Put to death men and woman, infant and nursing child, ox and sheep, camel and donkey.'"

So, Saul attacked the Amalekites. But he and the people spared Agog, the king of the Amalekites, and the best of the sheep, the oxen, the fatlings, the lambs, and all that was good, and were unwilling to destroy them. But everything they despised as worthless, they utterly destroyed (1Sam. 15:1-9).

Samuel said to Saul, "Listen to the voice of the words of Being. 'I will punish the Amalekites for how they ambushed Israelites on their way up from Egypt.'"

An Israelite coming out of Egypt: A person learning to "go" from dogma control to "go" to the Promised Earth. He can be easily confused and discouraged because he has not yet mastered the Soul Way.

Ambush: Let us consider one way that Dogmaites ambush a person seeking to be an Israelite.

Let us suppose that a person decides to leave the dogmas of a pharaoh to be guided primarily by Spirit. The rebel usually begins his exit by wandering in the wilderness because he has not discovered how to communicate all day, every day with Spirit to discover his answers. When a Dogmaite meets the lost soul, his false-love response is often to lead the confused person to another pharaoh and his dogmas. In that way, the Dogmaite "ambushes" the Israelite and leads him out of one form of slavery and into another.

Samuel said to Saul: "Now go and attack the Amalekites and utterly destroy them. Samuel said to Saul: Prevent Amalekites from brainwashing others with their dogmas.

Kill men and woman, infant and nursing children, ox and sheep, camel and donkey. (This is an allegory. To "kill" is not to destroy others physically, but to disrupt all Dogmaites, not just the leaders.)

This may appear to be an overly strong exhortation because, today, most do not recognize Dogmaites as dark disrupters. We even sometimes call their organizations, buildings, rituals, clothes, utensils, and dead bodies "holy" and "sacred." To make matters worse, we fund them through tax breaks and lift up their leaders as ideal champions of love and morality.

How Jesus Destroyed Dogmaites

Recall that Jesus was not fooled by dark indoctrinators who divide us (*The Gospel of Thomas*, Saying 16):

Perhaps
they
are thinking

[1]*Men*: Dogmaites.

Namely
men[1]

That
I
have come
to throw peace
upon the world;[2]

[2]*To throw peace upon the world*: To throw out comforting words to a Dogmaite world.

And
they
know
not

That
I
have come
to throw divisions
upon the earth:[3]

[3]*I have come to throw divisions upon the earth:* I have come to show the sharp difference between dark Dogmatites and light Israelites.

[4]*Fire:* Words that confront.

[5]*Sword:* Words that expose the difference between our false selves and real selves.

Fire[4]
sword[5]
and
war.[6]

[6]*War:* Words that cause a person's real self to fight his false self. Also, words that will cause division between those on the Mind Way and those on the Soul Way.

Jesus set out to save us by utterly destroying the Dogmaite groups that we call "sane," "normal," and "healthy." His weapons were his parables and sayings that first, show the danger of dogma identification; second, describe the goal of being wise-love in the Promised Earth; and third, teach the Soul Way for people to go from following pharaohs to following Spirit. By that strategy, he "attacks the Amalekites" (all Dogmaites) in a way that, over time, will "utterly destroy them."

So, Saul attacked the Amalekites. Thus, Saul prevented the Amalekites from causing problems for people who disagreed with their dogmas. For example, he may have stopped them from forcing others to obey their religious laws.

He took Agag, king of the Amalekites, alive, and utterly destroyed all the people with the edge of the sword. Saul found things to admire in Agag, the Dogmaite king, and decided to be his friend. Otherwise, he blocked his organization from imposing their dogmas on others.

Saul is in a bind. He needs money and warriors to suppress Dogmaite group rebellion. If he "utterly destroys" the Amalekite king, he will not possess his support to put down another group who disagrees with him. So, his strategy is to contain every dogma-based group while letting the rebel leaders continue to foment rebellion clandestinely.

Now the word of Being came to Samuel, saying, "I greatly regret that I have set up Saul as king, for he has turned back from following Me, and has not performed My commandments."

So, Samuel said to Saul: "Because you have rejected the word of Being, He also has rejected you from being king."

Therefore, Saul said to Samuel, "I have sinned, for I have transgressed the commandment of Being and your words because I feared the people and obeyed their voice."

Then, Being's comforting Spirit departed from Saul, and Being's distressing Spirit troubled him (1Sam. 15:1-16:14).

Now the word of Being came to Samuel, saying, "I greatly regret that I have set up Saul as king, for he has turned back from following Me, and has not performed My commandments." Spirit said through Samuel to Saul: "I am sorry I chose you as king because you have not taught people the darkness of the Mind Way and the light benefits of being on the Soul Way.

Therefore, Saul said to Samuel, "I have sinned, for I have transgressed the commandment of Being and your words." Saul said to Samuel. "I sinned when I did not point out unequivocally Dogmaite darkness and throw all of my support behind the Israelites."

Saul also said to Samuel. "I feared the people and obeyed their voice." Saul also said to Samuel, "I feared being rejected by my people and losing my kingship; and therefore, I did not condemn the Mind Way and teach the Soul Way.

Then, Being's comforting Spirit departed from Saul, and Being's distressing Spirit troubled him.

Two Spirits: As we saw in the Garden Allegory, Spirit always inspires us with a choice to evolve to higher levels of light or devolve to lower levels of darkness. If Spirit did not do that, we would be denied free choice. Some today call the inspiration to "go" to a higher level of love and wisdom "the Spirit of God." They call the source of inspiration to "go" to lower levels of life by such names as "Satan" and "the devil."

Being's distressing Spirit troubled Saul: Spirit led Saul into the Dark Experience so that he could learn the consequences of not living the Covenant. Jesus expresses this automatic, natural law in our being in *The Gospel of Thomas* (Saying 61):

When he should come to be divided,[1]	[1]*When he should come to be divided:* When King Saul came to be divided between his loyalty to Spirit and loyalty to Dogmaites…
He will be full of darkness.[2]	[2]*He will be full of darkness:* He was guided by Spirit to be full of the Dark Experience.

In this poem, Jesus expresses how Spirit wisely-loves us. When we choose to compromise—to try to be on the Soul and Mind Ways at the same time, our Guide will, in unconditional love, wisely give us what we want: Darkness. That is how Spirit teaches us the consequences of our choices.

Exercise:

Questions for Reflection: Saul chose to not "go" from which of the following false selves? (Mark each item below with a "No" or "Yes"):

1. His identification with his role as king.

2. His identification with his wealth and things.

3. His identification with those who support him.

4. His identification with his ego.

My answer: Saul did not choose to sacrifice any of these Isaacs (false identifications). Instead, He made them into his gods.

Buddha and False Identifications

Buddha (Ch. 13) captures Saul perfectly in the following poem:

Come
see the world,[1]

It
is
a painted chariot
for kings[2]
and
a snare
for fools.[3]

But
he
who sees the world
goes free.[4]

[1]*See the world:* Notice that everyone lives unconsciously from the beliefs of everyone else.

[2]*A painted chariot for kings:* An attractive, easy way for leaders like King Saul to enjoy himself.

[3]*A snare for fools:* A supposedly secure place where people can be fulfilled.

[4]*He who sees the world goes free:* He who perceives the dark world becomes free of Dogmaite kings like Saul and their minions.

Saul loved his chariot with all of its problems. He did not wish to set people free from the grip of Dogmaites.

Conclusion

Saul returned to his home with no intention of obeying Spirit and giving up his throne (1Sam. 15:34). Soon, he and his men were at war with the Philistines and other Dogmaite groups (1Sam. 17). As a result, Samuel did not see Saul again (1Sam. 15:35).

CHAPTER TWENTY-EIGHT

THE SAUL AND DAVID ALLEGORY: ISRAELITES DEFEAT GOLIATHS

SAMUEL SECRETLY APPOINTS ANOTHER KING

Being said to Samuel: "I send you to Jesse the Bethlehemite, for I have provided for myself a king among his sons."

Samuel visited Jesse and asked, "Are all your sons here?" And Jesse said, "There remains yet the youngest, but behold, he is keeping the sheep." And Samuel said to Jesse, "Send and fetch him."

Jesse brought him in. Now he was ruddy, had beautiful eyes, and he was handsome.

Being said to Samuel, "Arise, anoint him; for this is the one to be king."

Then Samuel took the horn of oil and anointed him amid his brothers, and the spirit of Being came mightily upon David from that day forward.

And Samuel rose up and went to Ramah, his home (1Sam. 16:1-13).

And Jesse said, "There remains yet my youngest (David), but behold, he is keeping the sheep."[15]

---

[15]   This David and Goliath section is patterned on the Cain and Able section of the Garden of Eden Allegory. See Appendix Four.

Sheep: An Israelite who has become pure by removing his garments (false selves).

A keeper of sheep: An Israelite leader who leads others on the Soul Way.

And Jesse said, "There remains yet my youngest (David), but behold, he is keeping the sheep." And Jesse said, "My youngest son, David, is not here because he is off wise-loving Israelites.

Being said to Samuel, "Arise, anoint him; for this is the one to be king." Spirit said to Samuel: "Wake up your intuition and notice that David is qualified to be my representative.

The spirit of Being came mightily upon David from that day forward. Spirit began to strongly guide David from that day forward until, as we shall see, he started listening to his ego-driven mind.

DAVID AND GOLIATH

> *Now the Philistines gathered together their army to battle. And Saul and the men of Israel gathered together. The Philistines stood on a mountain on the one side of a valley, and Israel stood on a mountain on the other side.*
>
> *The three eldest sons of Jesse went and followed Saul to the battle. So Jesse said to David, his son, "Take for your brothers a bushel of this parched corn and these ten loaves. And carry these ten pieces of cheese to the captain of their thousand men and find out if your brothers are well."*
>
> *And there went out a champion out of the camp of the Philistines, named Goliath, whose height was six cubits and a span. And he had a helmet of brass upon his head, and he was armed with a coat of mail. And he had leaves of brass upon his legs and a slab of brass between his shoulders. And the staff of his spear was like a weaver's beam, and his spear's head weighed six hundred shekels of iron. And he stood and cried out to the armies of Israel, "Choose a man for you and let him come down to me. If he can fight with me and kill me, then we*

will be your servants. But if I prevail against him and kill him, then you shall be our servants.

When Saul and all Israel heard those words of the Philistine, they were dismayed and greatly afraid.

And as David talked to his brothers, behold, Goliath, the champion, came up and challenged Saul and his army. And all the men of Israel, when they saw the man, fled from him and were very afraid.

And David asked the men, "Who is this uncircumcised Philistine that he should defy the armies of the living Gods?"

When Saul heard the words which David spoke, he sent for him. And David said to Saul, "Let no man's heart fail because of him. I, your servant, will go and fight with this Philistine.

And Saul said to David, You are not able to go against this Philistine to fight with him, for you are but a youth, and he a man of war from his youth.

And David said to Saul, "Being has delivered me out of the paw of a lion; therefore, he will deliver me out of the hand of this Philistine."

And Saul said to David, "Go and Being be with you."

Saul armed David with his armor, including putting a helmet of brass upon his head. Also, he armed him with a coat of mail. But David said unto Saul, "I cannot go with these; for I have not practiced within them. So, David removed them from him.

David then took his staff in his hand and chose five smooth stones out of the brook. He put them in a shepherd's bag. After putting his sling in his hand, he drew near to the Philistine.

When the Philistine looked, he saw David and disdained him, for he was but a youth, and ruddy, and of a fair countenance. And the Philistine cursed David by his gods.

Then, David said to the Philistine, "You come to me with a sword, spear, and shield: but I come to you in the name of Being and the armies of Israel, whom you have defied.

Later, the Philistine arose and came to meet David. Then, David put his hand in his bag, took out a stone, slung it, and smote the Philistine in his forehead, making him fall upon his face on the land. David, then, ran and stood upon the Philistine and took his sword, and slew him by cutting off his head.

When the Philistines saw that their champion was dead, they fled. And the men of Israel arose, shouted, and pursued the Philistines as far as the entrance of the valley.

Then, Saul took David that day and would not let him go back home to his father's house (1Sam. 17:1-18:2).

Now the Philistines gathered together their army to battle. The Philistines stood on a mountain on the one side of a valley, and Israel stood on a mountain on the other side. Now, the Dogmaite Philistines stood on their mountain, listening to their dogma-indoctrinated minds while Saul's men stood on their mountain, listening to their indoctrinators (No one is on his mountain communicating with Spirit).

And there went out a champion out of the camp of the Philistines, named Goliath, whose height was six cubits and a span. And a huge Dogmaite champion (e.g., a famous theologian like Thomas Aquinas, a noted philosopher like Karl Marx, or another influential dogma-leader) went out in front of his obedient, unconscious followers.

And he had a helmet of brass upon his head, and he was armed with a coat of mail. And he had leaves of brass upon his legs and a slab of brass between his shoulders. And he layered himself in impregnable garments (false selves).

And the staff of his spear was like a weaver's beam, and his spear's head weighed six hundred shekels of iron. And he possessed the necessary rhetoric to conquer all other Dogmaite champions.

And he stood and cried out to the armies of Israel, "Choose a man for you and let him come down to me. If he is able to fight with me and to kill me, then we will be your servants. But if I prevail against him and kill him, then you shall be our servants. And the Dogmaite champion challenged one of Saul's champions to a dogma debate with the understanding that the loser's institution would surrender.

When Saul and all Israel heard those words of the Philistine, they were dismayed and greatly afraid. When another Dogmaite institution challenged Saul and his Dogmaites, they trembled in fear because they did not possess an equally qualified spokesperson to argue their dogmas.

And David said to Saul, "Let no man's heart fail because of him. I, your servant, will go and fight with this Philistine. David said to Saul: "Do not be afraid because I will fight Goliath with my Soul Way wisdom."

And Saul said to David, "You are not able to go against this Philistine to fight with him, for you are but a youth, and he a man of war from his youth. Saul said to David, "You cannot fight a Dogmaite champion because you do not possess sufficient education and training on the Mind Way."

And David said to Saul, "Being has delivered me out of the paw of a lion; therefore, he will deliver me out of the hand of this Philistine. And David said to Saul, "Some time ago, Spirit inspired me to conquer another leading Dogmaite; therefore, Spirit will enable me to see through the reasoning of Goliath."

And Saul said to David, "Go, and Being be with you." And Saul said to David, "'Go' from us who are divided Dogmaites and 'go' with Spirit guidance to conquer Goliath."

Saul armed David with his armor, and he put a helmet of brass upon his head. Also, he armed him with a coat of mail. Saul armed David with false selves and their supporting dogmas.

But David said unto Saul, "I cannot go with these; for I have not practiced within them. So David removed them from himself. David said, "I have not been wearing garments (false selves) that make me weak. I will go as my naked, divine-life self."

THE OPPONENTS

GOLIATH	DAVID
A Dogmaite warrior	An Israelite warrior
Armored with his identification with his dogmas	Naked because he identifies with nothing but himself and Spirit
An adult-adult	An adult-child
In the world.	In the Promised Earth (Garden, Nirvana, Kingdom).

David, then, took his staff in his hand and chose five smooth stones out of the brook, and put them in a shepherd's bag which he had; and his sling was in his hand. Then, he drew near to the Philistine. David armed himself with the wisdom ("stones") taught to him by Spirit. He then marched to meet the Dogmaite champion.

David put his hand in his bag, and took out a stone, and slung it, and smote the Philistine in his forehead. David selected an appropriate stone (wise word, saying, or parable) and slung it at the forehead (mental dogmas) of Goliath.

And he fell upon his face to the land. And the Dogmaite became confused and sank deeper into his dark, semi-consciousness.

Then, David ran and stood upon the Philistine and took his sword, and slew him by cutting off his head. Then, David stood on his principles above the Dogmaite champion and visibly destroyed his standing in his world.

And when the Philistines saw their champion was dead, they fled. And when the Dogmaites realized that their champion's dogmas did not provide salvation, they retreated in fear and confusion.

And the men of Israel arose, shouted, and pursued the Philistines. And Saul's Dogmaites attacked the opposing Dogmaite institution.

Then, Saul took David that day and would not let him go back home to his father's house. Then, the Dogmaite Saul so realized that he needed the power and wisdom of the Israelite, David, that he demanded that the young man serve him.

CHAPTER TWENTY-NINE

THE SAUL AND DAVID ALLEGORY: DO NOT LOVE UNWISELY

David went out wherever Saul sent him and was successful in battle. Therefore, Saul set him over his warriors (1Sam. 18:5).

When David was returning from the slaughter of the Philistines, the women came out of all cities of Israel, singing and dancing to meet King Saul. And the women answered one another as they played, and said,

"Saul slew thousands, and

David tens of thousands."

As a result, Saul became angry because the woman's sayings displeased him. He said aloud, "They have ascribed to David tens of thousands, and to me, only thousands. He has everything but the kingdom."

So Saul became afraid of David because Being was with him and had departed from himself (1Sam. 18:5-16).

So Saul became afraid of David because Being was with him but had departed from himself. Saul became jealous and fearful of David rather than learn from him. As a result, Saul now lives a cursed life because he did not "eat" the wisdom of David. Jesus described that situation in his lion poem (*The Gospel of Thomas*: Saying 7):

And
he
is cursed[1]

[1]*And he is cursed:* And Saul is made miserable in the Dark Experience.

Namely
the man[2]

[2]*Namely, the man:* Namely the King who chooses to be jealous of an Israelite.

The one

That
the lion
will eat[3]

[3]*The one that the lion will eat:* The King Dogmaite that David will slowly destroy with his logic and presence.

And
the lion
comes to be
the man.[4]

[4]*And the lion comes to be the man:* And the spirit of David will come to haunt the terrified King Saul (as we will see).

THE ISRAELITE MARRIAGE OF DAVID AND MICHAL

Saul's daughter, Michal, was in love with David, and when Saul heard that, he was pleased. "I will give her to him," he thought, "so that she may be a snare to him (into leading the army) and so that the hand of the Philistines may slay him." Therefore, Saul said to David: "You shall now be my son-in-law" (1Sam. 18:20-28).

DAVID TRIES TO CHANGE SAUL

Because the Philistines were not able to kill David Saul took three thousand able young men from all Israel and set out to look for David.

Saul came to the sheep pens along the way and found a cave. He went in to relieve himself and did not know that David and his men were far back in the cave.

The men said to David, "This is the day Being spoke of when he said to you, 'I will give your enemy into your hands for you to deal with as you wish.'"

He said to his men, "Forbid that I should do anything harmful to my master, Being's anointed." With these words, David sharply rebuked his men and did not allow them to attack Saul.

Saul left the cave and went his way.

Then David went out of the cave and called out to Saul, "My lord, the king!" When Saul looked behind him, David bowed down and prostrated himself with his face to the ground.

He said to Saul, "Why do you listen when men say, 'David is bent on harming you'? This day you have seen with your own eyes how Being delivered you into my hands in the cave. Some urged me to kill you, but I spared you. I said, 'I will not lay my hand on my lord, because he is Being's anointed.' I have not wronged you, but you are hunting me down to take my life."

When David finished saying this, Saul asked, "Is that your voice, David, my son?" And he wept aloud.

"You are more righteous than I," Saul said. "You have treated me well, but I have mistreated you. You have just now told me about the good you did to me. Being delivered me into your hands, but you did not kill me. May Being reward you well for the way you treated me today. I know that you will surely be king and that the Kingdom of Israel will be established in your hands (1Sam. 24:2-20).

EXERCISE:

A QUESTION FOR REFLECTION: If you were David, would you have spared Saul's life or killed him?

MY ANSWER: Recall Being's command: "Now go and attack the Amalekites, and utterly destroy them."

Amalekites are Dogmaites. Saul became a Dogmaite, especially when he chose to kill him out of jealousy.

Israelites, like David, must "utterly destroy" Dogmaites, like Saul. The problem: everyone is, to some degree, an Israelite and a Dogmaite.

We Dogmaites are ego-bound to our false-god selves. When those demons are out of our control, we divide from others by seeing ourselves as good and them as bad—which automatically leads us to discriminate against, psychological and physically persecute, and even kill people (look at the religious conflicts in the world today).

We Dogmaties can be utterly destroyed in two ways:

- Each of us can continually identify our false selves and sacrifice those Isaacs, or

- Others need to limit and undermine our harmful impact on others.

Members of religions and political parties are both Dogmaites and Israelites. When we donate or give tax-breaks to their parent organizations, we not only do not utterly destroy them, we nurture them. That leads to further hateful division—often in the name of god, love, truth, and order.

What did David do? Instead of unconditionally loving Saul AND limiting and undermining his danger, he tried to change him by being nice to him. That is like an abused woman preparing a delicious meal for her husband, hoping, that he will stop beating and raping her. That is naïve love, not wise-love.

David, if he had lived 2500 years later, could have learned from an Israelite, Joan of Arc. She listened to Spirit, who guided her to give herself heroically to the service of her king and the Roman Catholic Church. She then did not hide in the hills from those jealous Dogmaites. As a result, they burned her at the stake.

When we choose to be Dogmaites, we become dangerous. At those times, unless we utterly destroy our false identities, only Israelites in wise-love can save themselves and the world from our love-hatred.

THE SITUATION

David has, in the moment, become a Dogmaite. He identifies with naïve love thinking that that will give him love and what he wants.

Saul, in the moment, has chosen to be a Dogmaite. He lives guarded-love. He guards himself first and loves only on the condition that others meet his needs.

Neither David nor Saul chose to be wise-love in the world: to both unconditionally love another, and at the same time, identify and guard oneself from the other's limitations—which always exist.

Now we will see who will win when naïve love meets guarded love.

SAUL'S TREACHERY

One night Saul sent messengers to David's house to watch him, that he might kill him in the morning. But Michal, David's wife, told him, "If you do not save your life tonight, tomorrow you will be killed." So, Michal let David down through the window, and he fled away and escaped (1Sam. 19: 11-12).

In retaliation, Saul gave Michal to Paltiel, son of Laish.

Then, David married two women, Abigail and Ahinoam (1Sam. 25:42-44).

SAUL'S DEATH

The Philistines fought against Israel. The battle pressed hard upon Saul. The Philistine archers found him and badly wounded him. Then, Saul said to his armor-bearer, "Draw your sword, and thrust me through with it, to prevent these uncircumcised to stab and make sport of me." But his armor-bearer would not, for he was very afraid. Therefore Saul took his sword and fell upon it. Thus Saul died along with his three sons, and his armor-bearer, and all his men, on the same day together (1Sam. 31:1-6).

CHAPTER THIRTY

THE KING DAVID ALLEGORY: REMAIN HUMBLE AND SINGLE

DAVID SETTLES IN HEBRON

David inquired of Being: "Shall I go up to one of the towns of Judah?" Being said, "Go up to Hebron." So David went up with his two wives (2Sam. 2:1-2).

Being said to David: "Go up to Hebron." After Saul died, Spirit guided David to go to Hebron, the city where Samuel, the last great Israelite prophet lived, and where the last large Israelite community survived in the Promised Earth. (Today, Hebron is a Palestinian city in the southern West Bank, 30 km south of Jerusalem, nestled in the mountains.)

DAVID UNITES ISRAEL

Ishbosheth, son of Saul, was forty years old when he became king over Israel, and he reigned two years. The tribe of Judah, however, remained loyal to David (2Sam. 2:10).

There was a long war between the house of Saul and the house of David; and David grew stronger and stronger, while the house of Saul became weaker and weaker.

At an advantageous point, David sent messengers to Ishbosheth, saying, "Give me my wife Michal, whom I married."

Ishbosheth, (afraid of David's power,) decided to take Michal from her husband and give her to David (2Sam. 3:1-15).

In Hebron, David reigned over Judah seven years and six months with his three wives and six sons (2Sam. 5:1-5).

DAVID ABANDONS THE COVENANT

One day, King David and his men went to Jerusalem and attacked the Jebusites who lived there. David captured the fortress of Zion and took up residence in it. He called it "The City of David."

Gradually, he became more and more powerful because Being-Gods were with him.

Now, Hiram king of Tyre sent envoys to David along with cedar logs and carpenters and stonemasons, and they built a palace for David.

Then David knew that Being had established him as King over Israel and had exalted his kingdom for the sake of his people Israel.

Then, David took more concubines and wives in Jerusalem. Thirteen more sons and daughters were born to him (2Sa 5:6-13) (1Chr.14:1-6).

King David and his men went to Jerusalem to attack the Jebusites, who lived there. Without being told by Spirit, David attacked the Jebusites in Jerusalem who posed no threat to the Israelites. Up until then, Saul and David put down Dogmaites who wanted to impose their dogmas on others. Now, David goes to war to steal the resources of others and to impose his religion and laws on them.

David captured the fortress of Zion and took up residence in it. Then, he called it "The City of David." Even though Spirit told him to live in Hebron surrounded by Israelites, David chose to live among Dogmaites in the fortress of Zion in Jerusalem. Then, to enhance his ego, he named the city after himself: "The City of David."

And he became more and more powerful because Being-Gods were with him. Like Moses, David became delusional. He justified his rise in power as the will of a God that he knows with the Tree of the Knowledge of Good and Bad.

Now Hiram king of Tyre sent envoys to David, along with cedar logs and carpenters and stonemasons, and they built a palace for David. David decides to divide himself even more from his people by building a palace to ensure that they adore him.

And David took more concubines and wives in Jerusalem. Thirteen more sons and daughters were born to him. And David grew more narcissistic, as evidenced by his sexual and psychological abuse of women and his lack of care for so many children.

JESUS EXPLAINS DAVID'S DARK DIVISION

David was powerfully one with Spirit when he fought Goliath. Then, his success and wealth went to his head. That *divided* him from Spirit, his real self, and the soul-self in others.

Jesus' explains how we become single in the Light Experience and divided in the Dark Experience in *The Gospel of Thomas* (Saying 61):

When
he
should come to be
destroyed[1]

[1]*When he should come to be destroyed:* When he should come to destroy his false selves (his ego),

He
will be full
of light.[2]

[2]*He will be full of light:* He will be single, that is, full of divine light.

When
however
he
should come to be
divided[3]

[3]*When, however, he should come to be divided:* When one should come to be divided between his real and false selves and between his real self and the real selves of others...

He
will be full
of darkness.[4]

[4]*He will be full of darkness:* He will be full of living death.

David desires fulfillment in the Promised Earth. To live there, he must "destroy" his ego and become "single"—one with himself. Instead of doing that, he chooses to live increasingly divided between his real self and his false identities, and between himself and others. So, more and more, he enjoys the Dark Experience outside of the Promised Earth.

In *The Gospel of Thomas* (Saying 22) Jesus explains that, unlike David, when we identify with nothing, we become single, not divided:

Jesus
peered upon some little-
ones
taking milk

And
he
said to his disciples:

"These little-ones
taking milk[1]

[1]*Little-ones taking milk:* People on the Soul Way who drink-in moment-to-moment Spirit guidance.

They
are comparable
to those

[2]*They are comparable to those who will go into the Kingdom:* They are those who will go into the Light Experience (Garden of Eden, Promised Earth, Nirvana).

Who
go inward
to the Kingdom?"[2]

The disciples
responded:

Then
we
being
little-ones

[3]*Then, we being little-ones, we will go inward to the Kingdom?* Then, because we follow you around like little children, we will go into the Kingdom?

We
will go inward
to the Kingdom?"[3]

Jesus
responded:

"When
you
should make the two
the one;[4]

And if
you
should make the side
inward
like
the side
outward

And
the side outward
like
the side inward

And
the side
upper
like
the side
lower[5]

And
not
the male
comes to be
a male

And so
you
will be making your
maleness
and
your femaleness
one
and
single

[4]*When you should make the two the one.* Jesus replied, "No, you need to do more than follow me around to be in the Kingdom. You need to leave your false selves and become "one" with your real self.

[5]*When you should make the side:"* To enter the Kingdom, you do not identify with any of your racial, class, intelligence, faith, etc. sides.

Such that
not
the female
comes to be
a female;[6]

And when
you
should make an eye
in place
of some eyes[7]

And
a hand
in place
of a hand[8]

And
a foot
in place
of a foot[9]

And
an appearance
in place
of an appearance;[10]

Then
you
will go inward
to the Kingdom."[11]

[6]*And so, you will be making your maleness and your femaleness one and single:* And so, to enter the Kingdom, you do not identify even with your gender. (You must see that men and women are soul-identical).

[7]*And when you should make an eye in place of some eyes:* And when you do not identify with your single-eye intuition or your two-eyed reasoning.

[8]*And when you should make a hand in place of a hand:* A "hand" signifies "control." And when you do not identify with being in control or out of control of the situation.

[9]*And when you should make a foot in place of a foot:* A "foot" signifies "the principles and beliefs that we stand on." And when you do not identify with your principles and beliefs.

[10]*And when you should make an appearance in place of an appearance:* And when you do not identify with how others perceive and judge you...

[11]*Then you will go inward to the Kingdom:* Then, being free of false selves and all the anger, frustration, depression, anxiety, and worry that you have caused by defending and promoting them, you will become the joyful, wise ruler of yourself and your interactions with others.

Buddha and Fools like David

Buddha comments on people like David in the following poem (Ch. 5):

"My children,
my wealth!"

With those thoughts
the fool
troubles himself.

For
he
has
not children
or wealth

When
he
is
not his own master.

The fool
who
knows that

Is
wise.

The fool

Who
believes that
he
is
wise,

He
is
a fool's fool.

Conclusion:

David has devolved to become a fool king. He has a dark kingdom but not the light kingdom he seeks. As a result, he is divided, not single. He has everything and nothing.

CHAPTER THIRTY-ONE

THE KING DAVID ALLEGORY: FOLLOW THE COVENANT IN YOUR ARK (HEART)

DAVID EXPROPRIATES THE COVENANT

One day, David assembled all Israel at Jerusalem to bring up the Ark of Being to its place there, which he had prepared for it.

Then David said, "No one but the Levites may carry the ark of God, for Being chose them to carry the Ark of Being and to minister to him forever."

David also commanded the chiefs of the Levites to appoint their brethren as the singers who should play loudly on musical instruments, on harps and lyres and cymbals, to raise sounds of joy.

David was clothed with a robe of fine linen, as also were all the Levites who were carrying the ark, and the singers, and Chenanah, the leader of the music of the singers (1Chr.15: 1-27).

And as the Ark of Being came into the city of David, Michal, Saul's daughter and David's wife, when she looked through a window and saw King David leaping and dancing before Being, she despised him in her heart.

David, then, blessed the people in the name of Being. When he returned to bless his household, Michal, the daughter of Saul and his wife, came out to meet David. She said, "How glorious was the king of Israel today, who undressed himself today in full view of the slave girls as any vulgar man shamelessly undresses!"

David said to Michal, "It was before Being who chose me rather than your father or anyone from his house when he appointed me ruler over the people of Israel; therefore, I will play before Being.

I will become even viler than this, and I will be humiliated in my own eyes. But by these slave girls you spoke of, I will be held in honor."

Therefore, Michal had no child unto the day of her death (2Sa 6:15-23).

One day, David assembled all Israel at Jerusalem to bring up the Ark of Being to its place, which he had prepared for it. One day, David called together all of the Dogmaites and Israelites living in Israel to celebrate the move of the Ark of the Covenant to his city to be under his control.

THE SITUATION

Recall that the Ark is a symbol of one's heart in which is written the Covenant. So the Ark belongs to everyone equally. That is why in Israel's Golden Age, the people moved it around from place to place. They never associated it with a secular government.

Now, David moves the Ark to his capital, which tells the people, symbolically, "Now, I will control the thoughts and actions that flow from your heart. Being will speak to you through me." In that way, David becomes the tyrant twin of Moses and ends the Israelite Golden Age.

Then David said, "No one but the Levites may carry the Ark of God, for Being chose them to carry the Ark of Being and to minister to Him forever. David also commanded the chiefs of the

Levites to appoint their brethren as the singers who should play loudly on musical instruments, on harps and lyres and cymbals, to raise sounds of joy." David, like Moses, sets up a hierarchy of sub-pharaohs to carry out his will over the people.

David was clothed with a robe of fine linen, as also were all the Levites who were carrying the Ark, and the singers, and Chenaniah, the leader of the music of the singers. David and his sub-pharaohs and their staff divided themselves further from the people by wearing distinctive garments (false selves).

As the Ark of Being came into the city of David, Michal, Saul's daughter and David's wife, when she looked through a window and saw king David leaping and dancing before Being, despised him in her heart. When David brought the Ark to his capital, Michal saw that he was substituting his dictatorial commandments and laws for Spirit's guidance. She, therefore, despised him.

Then, David blessed the people in the name of Being. Then, David decided to raise himself above the people even more by claiming that he is authorized to bless them in the name of Spirit.

When he returned to bless his household, Michal, the daughter of Saul and his wife, came out to meet David. She said, "How glorious was the king of Israel today, who undressed himself today in full view of the slave girls of his servants, as any vulgar fellow shamelessly undresses!" Michal, the Israelite, confronted David for the way he dishonored and demeaned himself and Spirit.

David said to Michal, "It was before Being, who chose me rather than your father or anyone from his house when he appointed me ruler over the people of Being, over Israel; therefore, I will play before Being. I will become even viler than this, and I will be humiliated in my own eyes. But by these slave girls you spoke of, I will be held in honor." In his response to Michal, David justifies and brags about his self-righteousness.

Therefore, Michal had no child until the day of her death. Therefore, Michal would no longer be sexually intimate with David because he had corrupted the Israelite Covenant.

DAVID ESTABLISHES HIS GOVERNMENT

So David reigned over all Israel by administering justice and equity to all his people. And Joab the son of Zeruiah was over the army, and Jehoshaphat, the son of Ahilud, was recorder; and Zadok the son of Ahitub and Ahimelech the son of Abiathar were priests; and Shavsha was secretary; and Benaiah, the son of Jehoiada, was over the Cherethites and the Pelethites; and David's sons were the chief officials in the service of the king (and there follows a long list of subordinates) (1Chr.18:14-16).

Over time, David defeated the Philistines and subdued them, and he took Gath and its surrounding villages from the control of the Philistines. He also defeated the Moabites, and they became subject to him and brought him tribute. Moreover, David defeated Hadadezer king of Zobah, in the vicinity of Hamath. He then captured a thousand of his chariots, seven thousand charioteers, and twenty thousand foot soldiers. He hamstrung all but a hundred of the chariot horses. When the Arameans of Damascus came to help Hadadezer king of Sabah, David struck down twenty-two thousand of them. He put garrisons in the Aramean kingdom of Damascus, and the Arameans became subject to him and brought him tribute. Thus, David reigned over all Israel, doing what was just and right for all his people (1Ch. 18:1-14).

So, David reigned over all Israel by administering justice and equity to all his people. So, David, like Moses and Saul, tyrannically brought about justice and peace to those who agree with him and his interpretation of the Torah Laws, and horrific suffering to those who did not.

DAVID COMMISSIONS THE FIRST TEMPLE AND JUDAISM

David said, "The house that we will build for Being must be exceedingly magnificent, presenting our fame and glory throughout all lands. I will, therefore, prepare for it."

David said to Solomon, "My son, I had it in my heart to build a house to the name of the Being-Gods. But the word of Being came to me, saying, 'You shall not build a house to my name, because you have shed so much blood before me upon the land. Behold, a son shall be born to you; he shall be a man of peace. He shall build a house for my name.

"Now, my son, Being be with you so that you may succeed in building the house of the Being-Gods, as he has spoken concerning you. Only, may Being grant you discretion and understanding that when he gives you charge over Israel, you may keep the law of Being-Gods. Then you will prosper if you are careful to observe the statutes and the ordinances which Being commanded Moses for Israel."

"With great pains, I have provided for the house of Being a hundred thousand talents of gold, a million talents of silver, and bronze and iron beyond weighing, for there is so much of it; timber and stone too, I have provided. To these, you must add. You also have an abundance of workmen: stonecutters, masons, carpenters, and all kinds of craftsmen (1Chr.22: 1-18)."

David said, "The house that we will build for Being must be exceedingly magnificent, of fame and glory throughout all lands.

House: A "house" is "a way of being." So:

A person can be a "house." He can be a "divided house" when he is divided between his real and false selves. Or he can be an "empty house" when he is empty of false selves.

A tribe or family can also be a house when everyone lives by the same principles and beliefs. It also can be divided or unified.

A temple, mosque, a church or any other building can be a house when it symbolizes the principles and beliefs of the people who meet there. It also can be divided or unified.

Those living on the Soul Way are in one unified house. Those on the Mind Way are in a divided house.

David said, "The house that we will build for Being must be exceedingly magnificent, of fame and glory throughout all lands. David said: "The temple that we Dogmaites will build for Spirit must be so magnificent that it both glorifies my people and me and places us apart and over all other peoples." Or, "Our house must be a symbol of division in the world, not unity."

Buddha and the Fool's House

Buddha (Ch. 5) composed a poem that aptly describes David's house:

A fool (like David)
wants recognition,
a position (house)
before other people,
a position (house)
over other people.

"Let them
appreciate my work,

Let everyone
seek direction from me,"

Such
are
his wishes,

Such
is
his swelling pride.

One Way
(of Darkness)
leads to wealth
and fame,

The other
(of light)
to the end
of the Way
(of the Soul).

BACK TO THE ALLEGORY

But the word of Being came to me (David), saying, "You shall not build a house to my name, because you have shed so much blood before me upon the land." Spirit told David, "You shall not build a house signifying my Soul Way because you have used the Tree of the Knowledge of Good and Bad to cause so much death in yourself and my people.

David said to Solomon, "You will prosper if you are careful to observe the statutes and the ordinances which Being commanded Moses for Israel. David said to Solomon: "You and our people will prosper if you *ignore* both Abraham's Covenant and the Garden Command, and instead, you observe the Ten Commandments and the Mosaic laws." (See Appendix Four).

THE AFTERMATH

Solomon built the First Temple. It was in Judea; consequently, the members of that house then and today are called "Jews," and their religion is called "Judaism.

The king of the Neo-Babylonian Empire, Nebuchadnezzar II, destroyed Solomon's Temple in 586 BCE. After conquering Jerusalem, the king sent part of the population of the Kingdom of Judah into exile to Babylon. When the Jews returned in about 516 BCE, they built the Second Temple. That survived until the Romans destroyed it in 70 CE.

According to the Abraham allegory, metaphorically, everyone in the world is a Dogmaite or an Israelite. In other words, each of us is a house dirty with dogma or one cleansed of dogma. When a person is in the Light Experience on the Soul Way, he is the 3rd cleansed temple.

CHAPTER THIRTY-TWO

THE BOOK SUMMARY

INTRODUCTION

We have been learning about the revolutionary "Soul Way" that was taught by Eve, Abraham, Buddha, and Jesus. As we discovered, it is almost entirely unknown today because few organizations teach it. It is an emotional health and spiritual development methodology. We contrasted it with the "Mind Way," which causes most of our personal, group, and global conflicts. This chapter breaks the summary of what we have concluded into three parts:

1. The *foundational principles* of the Soul Way and the Mind Way,

2. The *process* of leaving the Mind Way to live on the Soul Way, and

3. The *goal* of living on the Soul Way.

THE FOUNDATIONAL PRINCIPLES OF THE TWO WAYS

DOGMAITES ON THE MIND WAY	ISRAELITES ON THE SOUL WAY
Are descendants of indoctrinators like Moses, Saul, David, Solomon, Paul the Apostle, and Mohammed.	Are descendants of liberators like Eve, Abraham, Buddha, Jesus, Jacob, Joseph, Joshua, and Samuel.
Are primarily governed by religious and secular laws and beliefs.	Primarily make the Garden Command and Abraham's Covenant more important than religious or secular laws.

They communicate with Spirit in a dogma-contaminated temple, church, or mosque.	They are the cleansed-of-dogma 3rd Temple in which they continually communicate with Spirit.
Dogma-based leaders teach them their personal answers.	They discover their personal answers.
They primarily use mental reasoning to arrive at their answers.	They primarily use soul-intuition (third-eye and ear knowing) to arrive at their answers
They eat of the Tree of the Knowledge of Good and Bad.	They eat of the Tree of the Knowledge of Life.
They live in the Dark Experience (in Nod, the Wilderness, and in the World).	They live in the Light Experience (in the Garden of Eden, the Promised Earth, Nirvana, and in the Kingdom).
They are divided from the soul essence of themselves and others.	They unite with the soul essence of themselves and others.
They live in the past and future on a roller coaster of emotions	They live in the present in stillness, joy, and peace.
They long for peace in an "age" when everyone else adopts their dogmas.	They long for peace in an "age" when no one lives from conflicting dogmas, and everyone continually discovers their unique answers.
They know that the perception of truth is the same for everyone.	They know that the perception of truth depends on the level of wise-love lived by a person.
Because they see luck and coincidence in the universe, they seek safety in things and people and pray for divine intervention.	Because they see perfect order in the universe, they peacefully reveal their next step and never pray for divine intervention.

The Process: From the Mind Way to the Soul Way

Jesus summarized the developmental process that a person goes through when he leaves the Mind Way to live all day, every day on the Soul Way in a mini-allegory from *The Gospel of Thomas* (Saying 98):

The Kingdom
of the Father[1]

[1] *The Kingdom of the Father:* Jesus' term for the Light Experience (The Garden of Eden, the Promised Earth, and Nirvana).

It
is comparable
to a woman[2]

[2] *An Israelite* (Such as Eve, Abraham, Jacob, Joseph, and Joshua, Buddha, and Jesus).

She
bearing a jar[3]

[3] *Jar:* One's ego.

It
full of meal[4]

[4] *Meal:* Food, that is, "fruit" of the Tree of the Knowledge of Good and Bad, which are false selves and their associated dogmas.

She
walking on a Way[5]

[5] *Way:* The Soul Way.

It
far away.[6]

[6] *Faraway:* The end of the Soul Way is "far away."

The ear[7]
of the jar
broke

[7] *The ear of the jar broke:* The Israelite woman began to rely on her intuitive third-ear rather than her reasoning two-ears.

And
the meal
emptied[8]
after her
along the Way,

[8] *The meal emptied after her along the Way:* She sacrificed her false selves along the Soul Way.

And
she
knew
not what
was happening[9]

[9] *She did not know what was happening:* Ultimately, the developmental process on the Soul Way is a mystery and a miracle.

And
she
did
not realize any trouble.[10]

[10]*She did not realize any trouble:* She enjoyed the hard work of sacrificing herself of her false selves.

When
she
opened inward
to her house[11]

[11]*She opened inward to her house:* She looked inside herself.

She
released the jar
down[12]

[12]*She released the jar down:* She stopped carrying herself full of false selves and the need to defend and promote their associated dogmas.

And
she
discovered it
empty.[13]

[13]*She discovered it empty:* She no longer possessed an ego. Now, she can enjoy life in the Light experience without being on a rollercoaster of dark emotions.

Buddha (Ch. 25) also stated that an "empty house" is our goal:

With a still mind
come into your empty house
your heart
and feel the joy
of the Way
beyond the world.

THE GOAL OF THE SOUL WAY

As we grow on the Soul Way, we become more the "light" that our dark world needs. As we do that, we increasingly can describe ourselves to ourselves in a powerful manner as described by Jesus in *The Gospel of Thomas* (Saying 77):

I
am
the light[1]

[1]*Light:* Divine life in the dark world of false selves.

The one

Which
is
upon them[2]

[2]*The one that is upon them:* The one who confronts them by being light.

All of them.
I
am
the All.[3]

[3]*I am the All:* I live the life that is in everyone and everything, even things that many regard as inanimate.

Has
the All
come outward
of me[4]

[4]*Has the All come outward of me:* Divine life and intelligence flow through me.

And
has
the All
split
to become me.[5]

[5]*And has the All split to become me:* And has divine life in All split itself to become my unique personality.

Split
a timber

And
I
am
there;

Take
the stone
up

And
you
will discover me
there.[6]

[6]*Split a timber, and I am there. Take a stone up, and you will discover me there.* When you peer on All with a single eye and listen to All with a single ear, you will see that I am the unique expression of the life in All.

When we grow on the Soul Way daily, we can experience ourselves as described in this poem. So, our goal is to become a "light," that is, wise-love of All in the world.

Buddha (Ch. 2) also saw that our goal is to be light to All:

Live on the Way

*And
the light
will evolve in you.*

THE SOUL WAY

THE MIND WAY

As we evolve, we become the light of wise-love of All in the world.

↑

As we devolve, we become the dark, false-love of All in the world.

APPENDIX ONE

ADDENDUM TO CHAPTER TWENTY-THREE

Eight times in the Book of Joshua (1:7-8; 8: 31, 32, 34; 22:5; 23:6; 24:26) we read statements like the following which seem to indicate that Joshua and his Israelites had abandoned the Covenant and had returned to making Moses' laws their false guide:

> *Only be strong and very courageous, being careful to do according to all the law which Moses my servant commanded you; turn not from it to the right hand or the left, that you may have good success wherever you go (Jos.1:7).*

I am rather certain that eight instances of a call to follow Torah Laws were inserted later by a scribe. I came to this conclusion because:

1. The insertions seem to interrupt the flow of the text.

2. The reminders do not follow instances where the Israelites were not following the Mosaic Laws.

3. The reminders are not followed by descriptions of consequences to those Israelites who did not follow the Torah Laws.

4. The insertions counter the concluding paragraph in the Book of Joshua that describes Joshua's death-bed exhortation for the Israelites to follow the Covenant: Joshua said: "Do not set aside the Covenant of Being-Gods which he commanded you to observe" (Josh. 23:16).

APPENDIX TWO

ABEL AND DAVID VS. CAIN AND SAUL

Early in Genesis, we read an allegory about Cain and Abel (Gen 4:2-8):

The man
knew his woman,

And
she
conceived

And
she
bore Cain;

And
she
said,

"I
have gotten a man
from Being."

And
she
again
bore his brother
Abel

Abel
was
a keeper
of sheep.

Cain
was
a tiller
of the earth.

In time
Cain
brought the fruit
of the earth
as
an offering
to Being.

Abel
brought the first-born
of his flock
and
its best part.

Being
respected Abel
with his offering.

For Cain
and
his offering

Being
had
no respect.

Cain
became furious

And
his face
fell.

When
in the field
Cain
rose up against his brother

And
murdered him.

One of the sons of the man and woman in the Garden Allegory was Abel. He was a "keeper of sheep" (a Wise-Lover of Israelites) on the Soul Way.

The man and woman also birthed another son, Cain. He "tilled the earth" because he lived in Nod on the Mind Way (Gen 3:23).

As we learned above, Cain, out of jealousy, murdered Abel (Gen 4:2-8).

The author of the Saul and David allegory used the Cain and Abel allegory as his template. David was also a "keeper of sheep." Like Cain, Saul chose to eat of the Tree of the Knowledge of Good and Bad, when out of jealousy, he tried to murder David.

CAIN AND SAUL	ABEL AND DAVID
Workers of the earth.	Keepers of sheep.
Led by their egos.	Led by Spirit.
Suffering jealousy and hatred in the Dark Experience.	Fulfilled in Wise-Love of All in the Light Experience.

APPENDIX THREE

DAVID AND THE TORAH LAWS

David said to Solomon, "You will prosper if you are careful to observe the statutes and the ordinances which Being commanded Moses for Israel (1Chr.22: 16-18).

David said to Solomon: "You and our people will prosper if you ignore both Abraham's Covenant and the Garden Command, and instead, you all observe the Ten Commandments and the Mosaic laws."

How did King David come to this point where he makes Moses' Dogmaite "statutes and ordinances" more important than his Israelite heritage?

There follows my conjecture about what happened:

1. Slowly, David devolved to becoming a narcissistic Saul, squared.

2. Out of love for himself and his people, David decided to rape and dominate the surrounding nations.

3. To ensure order and subservience to his will throughout his kingdom, David decided to write universal laws governing everyone.

4. To ensure that everyone obeys his laws, David decided to **embed them** in the treasured Moses Allegory. Those laws are now called the "Torah Laws." We have evidence that this happened because:

    a. When I applied Semitic Parallelism to the Moses Allegory, it disclosed the structure and meaning of the Allegory *except* where we read the Torah Laws. That is the primary reason to believe that a scribe inserted them after the composition of the Allegory.

b. The Torah Laws are not emphasized again in the later Joshua, Judges, or Saul allegories, because their authors never heard of them. If they were in the original Allegory, Joshua and others would have built their messages around them.

c. The Torah Laws contain vocabulary not found in the rest of the Moses Allegory nor in the later allegories. Again, if the Laws were in the original Allegory, the texts after it would be replete with the same language.

d. The Torah Laws contain prescriptions that Moses did not need to govern his people in the wilderness. For example, how to treat and sell slaves, even one's daughter. Those laws would not be in the original.

e. The Torah Laws contain highly detailed requirements for building a temple—something that people on the move in the wilderness did not need. However, if David wanted to administer burdensome taxes on the people to build such an elaborate edifice, he would meet less resistance if he could convince his subjects that Being through Moses demanded such a structure. So, it appears that he had his scribes insert his temple blueprints in the Moses Allegory.

f. At the places in the Moses Allegory where we read the Torah Laws, we notice an abrupt shift in mood and subject matter. I could not find a single instance of a smooth preface or conclusion to the Laws. The text reads as if a scribe in several places cut a previous, continuous manuscript and brutishly taped in the Torah Laws, some here, some there.

5. After inserting the Torah Laws in the Moses Allegory, David gave copies to all of his sub-pharaohs throughout the kingdom. He told them that they were to brainwash his subjects by retelling the Allegory repeatedly until they believed that disobedience to the laws would bring down punishment from Being-Gods, and obedience, great bounty.

The Result of David's Creation of the Torah Laws

1. David established a Dogmaite church-state with himself as the ruling god instead of Spirit.

2. David ensured that people worship his persona and will.

3. David once and for all decided to destroy the Israelite nation and Abraham's legacy utterly.

4. David established the conditions of continual Jewish holocausts. (What happens when in a playground a child goes to the high hill in the middle and declares himself the good, chosen king over others)?

5. David wrote large a model for glorious church-states that cause so much suffering today.

Further Research

I have just outlined my conjectures. Research by other historians and linguists is needed to provide more convincing evidence.

APPENDIX FOUR

NOTES ABOUT THE TRANSLATIONS

As I stated in the Preface, I discovered what appears to be the way that the Semitics organized their texts. I call this methodology, "Semitic Parallelism," and I explain it in my book, *The Semitic Secret, How Semitic Authors Organized Their Books to Include a Dictionary, Commentary, and a Method of Determining Copyist Errors.*[16] I used the principles of Semitic Parallelism to understand the meaning of the texts composed by Eve, Abraham, and Jesus.

I translated and interpreted the Garden of Eden story according to its structure. It can be found in my book, *The Semitic Secret.*

I also translated and interpreted *The Gospel of Thomas* according to its structure.[17] I used many interlinear translations, especially the one by Mike Grondin.[18]

For my translation of the Dhammapada, I used a variety of translations, especially one by Ven. Thanissaro, Bhikkhu.[19]

---

[16]   North, Robert William; *The Semitic Secret, How Semitic Authors Organized Their Books to Include a Dictionary, Commentary, and a method of determining Scribal Errors, The Soul Way Press, 2019. (Available only at www.7771.org).*

[17]   North, Robert William: *The Gospel of Thomas—The Original 21-Chapter Poetic Arrangement, The Soul Way Press, 2017. Because of the complex layout, the digital version can only be purchased at www.7771.org .*

[18]   *Grondin, Mike, An interlinear Coptic-English version of the Gospel of Thomas, (2000).*

[19]   *Thanissaro Bhikkhu, Tranalator, The Dhammapada, Buddha Dharma Education Association Inc.. The Path of Dhamma", edited by Access to Insight. Access to Insight (BCBS Edition), 30 November 2013,*

ACKNOWLEDGMENTS

My name is on the front of the book. I did the bulk of the work; however, I could not have finished the book without the support of others.

CRITICAL SUPPORTERS

Norman J. Bets, Sponsor and Book Editor

Don Talarico, Advisor and Style Editor

READERS WHO PROVIDED VALUABLE FEEDBACK

Joseph Rook

Jack Ewers

Steve Mitchell

CPSIA information can be obtained
at www.ICGtesting.com
Printed in the USA
LVHW020314140920
665930LV00019B/626